SIME BOOKS

Maria Castellano

Photographs by
Stefano Scatà

Illustrations by
Monica Parussolo

Mamma, let's cook!

Italian recipes to make with kids by il Gufo

The author dedicates this book to her mother and father. She would like to thank *Il Gufo* and Maria Luisa Gardiman for their confidence in her and young Albi and Sveva. Maria Luisa Gardiman thanks Emile Henry (www.emilehenry.com) and Alessandra Fior of *Fiorirà un giardino* (www.fioriraungiardino.com) for all the materials provided.

(c) SIME BOOKS

Sime srl
Viale Italia 34/E
31020 San Vendemiano (TV) - Italia
www.simebooks.com

This book is a special initiative
by Il Gufo.

Il Gufo spa
Chidren dressed as Children
Via G. Galilei 3/A
31011 Asolo (TV) - Italia
www.ilgufo.it

Recipes: Maria Castellano
Editing: William Dello Russo
Translation: Sarah Ponting and Chris Turner
Photographs: Stefano Scatà
Food stylist: Maria Luisa Gardiman
House master: Sabrina Volpato
Illustrations: Monica Parussolo
Design: Italo Meneghini – WHAT! design
Page make-up Giada Venturino
Post production cover: numerique.it
Post production images: Rodrigo Pivoto
Quality control: Fabio Mascanzoni
Acknowledgements: Jenny Biffis

Printed in Germany
Offizin Andersen Nexö Leipzig GmbH

ISBN 978-88-95218-17-5

Here we are, at last, at home with our children: in the kitchen and subsequently at the table, enjoying a deep intimacy in which we communicate, share and learn.

With the television and computer switched off, we discover and cherish the unique value of these moments of sharing that arise around the stove, preparing dough for pizza, cutting out pastry shapes, slicing mozzarella or stirring mashed potato.

We wish to convey to our children all the values that, together with love and respect for oneself and others, develop naturally with everyday activities, sport, music and play, in a healthy process that shapes a set of basic mores in which diet and cooking play a leading role.

For us, learning to eat and preparing food is the best start to a happy life, which is the reason why we devised this entertaining educational project, with a book of easy recipes whose quality is evident in every aspect: contents, pictures and, above all, flavors. We have put the same enthusiasm into it that we invest in our daily task of dressing children as children.

We dedicate it to mothers, grandmothers and friends. We dedicate it to our children and our grandchildren, and to the children of all those who wish to share this view of education and love of life.

Alessandra Chiavelli
Giovanna Miletti
Il Gufo

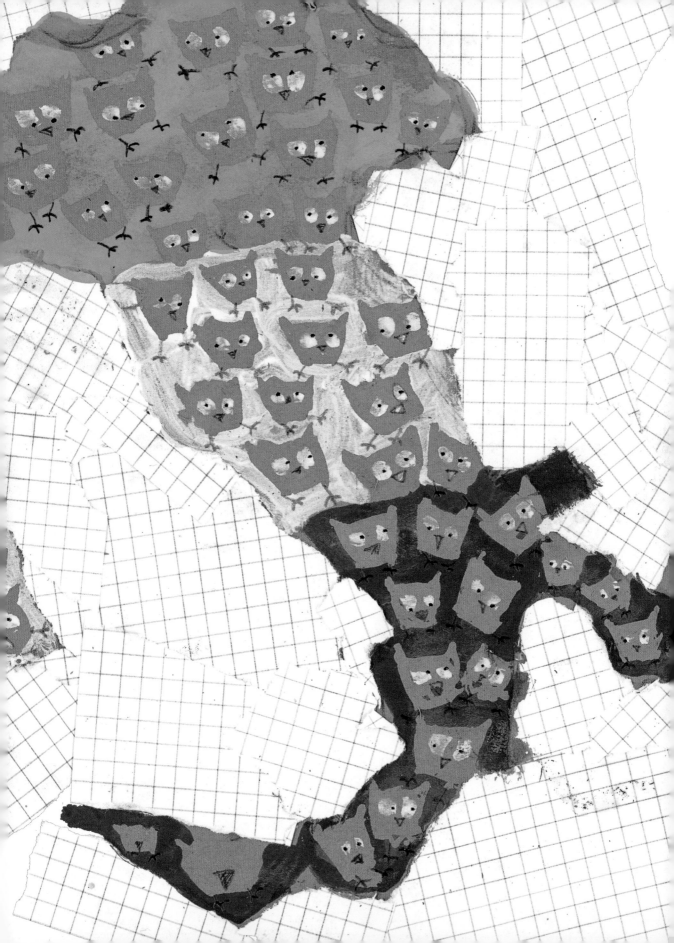

Parents and children in the kitchen, together: it's not an impossible feat, as this book aims to show you. If suitably encouraged, even the youngest children, can help adults to prepare simple and tasty recipes and become little chefs!

Maria Castellano will take you by the hand to accompany adults and children alike on a journey to discover Italy's unique recipes. Pasta, pizzas, fruit, vegetables, meat and fish: only the best of Italian cookery, in many delicious recipes! Their glories are magnified by the photographs by Stefano Scatà and the illustrations by Monica Parussolo.

All the dishes have been tested for children, whose palates have been considered in selecting the most natural ingredients, in the conviction that Italian cuisine is a lifestyle to be cultivated from childhood. Most of the recipes can be made together with children, who will not only enjoy crushing, mixing and tasting, but will also learn how to measure ingredients, coordinate the various stages and, not least, improve their reading, concentration and memory skills. They will learn to become familiar with kitchen utensils (and use them safely), basic techniques and cooking times. Eating dishes that they have prepared themselves will boost their self-confidence, gratify their palates and make them respect the fundamental value of food in the life of every man and woman.

Sime Books

Contents:

Recipe difficulty

 Very easy

 Easy

 Intermediate

 Challenging

Before starting

Setting the table

Setting the table is one of the happiest and most enthralling moments for children. You can delegate this task almost entirely to them, secure in the knowledge that they will perform it well. All children enjoy giving a personal touch to the finished table. You can also decide on the seating plan with them and make the place cards together.

Ten steps for a perfectly set table:

1 Carefully place the linen or cotton tablecloth on the tabletop, smoothing out any folds or lumps. Ensure that the same amount of fabric hangs down on each side.

2 Use a tablemat to place serving dishes on if wished.

3 Each place should have a plate, for the main course, and a bowl, for the starter.

4 Consider adding two smaller plates if you are going to serve an antipasto and fruit.

5 The napkin, co-ordinated with the tablecloth, should be folded and placed on the top plate.

6 A water glass should be set at each place and also a wine glass for adults.

7 Consider the number of courses to establish the amount of cutlery – forks, knives, spoons and teaspoons – required.

8 Pour still and sparkling water into separate pitchers, according to the number of guests.

9 Make a centerpiece if wished.

10 Arrange the place cards, alternating adults and children and people who do not know each other.

Children at table

Position.
Sit comfortably on your chair with your back straight.

Hands.
Rest your hands on the table, never your elbows.

Napkin.
Take your napkin from the table and spread it over your legs. Use only when necessary.

Cutlery.
Use cutlery for all food. Only bread and certain fruits may be eaten with your fingers.

Glasses.
Never clink glasses with cutlery.

Knives.
Avoid making grating noises with your knife on your plate.

Getting up.
Do not get up from the table between courses unless asked by an adult.

Voice.
Use a tone suitable for conversation and never raise your voice.

Opinions and compliments.
Never judge a dish before tasting it . . . and even if you do not like it, do not express your opinion.

Cell phones and videogames.
Cell phones and videogames should be left in your bedroom.

Cleanliness and tidiness

A clean, tidy kitchen ensures that each recipe is a success and saves the cook both time and energy. Preparing utensils and ingredients in advance makes following the various stages of preparation of dishes much easier and more efficient.

Here are the 5 basic rules to follow, for adults and children alike.

1 Wash and dry your hands thoroughly before starting to cook and wear an apron to protect your clothes.

2 Check in advance that you have all the utensils and accessories required by the recipe and that they are clean and ready to use.

3 Prepare all the necessary ingredients in advance, arranging them on a worktop according to their order of use.

4 Dispose of waste as you go along and put leftovers in the fridge.

5 As you work, wash up or put in the dishwasher the plates that you have used and no longer need.

Kitchen safety

The kitchen is a magical place: it is only there that previously separate ingredients are combined into delicious, colorful dishes. However, the kitchen can also become a "dangerous" place, full of enemies and perils. But never fear, there is no need to instill a terror of blades and boiling pans: children simply need to learn how to behave around them.

Just pay attention to our 10 basic safety rules, always ensuring that you give children clear instructions. And children, make sure that you always listen carefully to what adults tell you!

Use pointed and sharp objects like knives and scissors only under the supervision of an adult. Take care when using cheese graters too, always keeping your fingers at a safe distance.

Keep away from the oven when hot, as you can burn yourself simply by touching the glass. Stay away from griddles and burners too, as they remain hot even after use.

Always use oven gloves when removing dishes from the oven, and always with the help of an adult. Stay well away from hot burners and never allow your hair or clothes near them.

Never touch pans containing boiling water. Stay well away from pans during frying in order to avoid being splashed by boiling oil.

Be very careful with kitchen appliances like kneading machines, blenders or electric whisks, and use them only with an adult. Keep electrical appliances well away from the sink.

Sunday Brunch

Sparkling orange and pink grapefruit juice

Berry flying saucer

Pancakes with honey

Soft bread with butter and Strawberry jam

Omelette with ham, cheese and herbs

Spinach pie

Bruschetta with tomatoes, olives and capers

Hot chocolate

Sparkling orange and pink grapefruit juice

Preparation time: 5 minutes

Ingredients for 1 pitcher:
- 2 cups chilled carbonated water
- 2 oranges
- 2 pink grapefruits
- 4 fresh mint leaves

Preparation:

Cut the fruit in half and squeeze.

Pass the juice through a fine strainer.

Pour the filtered juice into a pitcher. Add the carbonated water and mint leaves.

Spremuta frizzante di arancia e pompelmo rosa

Berry flying saucer

Preparation time: 30 minutes - Cooking time: 55 minutes

Ingredients for 6 people:

- 2½ cups all-purpose flour
- 1½ tablespoons baking powder
- 4 eggs
- ⅞ cup fresh raspberries
- 1 cup soft butter
- 1½ cups sugar

Preparation:

Cream the butter and sugar until smooth.

Mix in the lightly beaten eggs.

When the mixture has expanded, gently fold in the flour combined with the baking powder.

Finally add the raspberries.

Pour the mixture into a greased and floured springform baking pan (9½" diameter).

Bake at 350°F for 55 minutes.

Disco volante ai frutti rossi

Pancakes
with honey

Preparation time: 20 minutes - Rising time: 30 minutes - Cooking time: 5 minutes

Ingredients for 20 pancakes:

- 1½ cups all-purpose flour
- 1½ tablespoons baking powder
- 2 eggs
- 1 cup milk
- 1¾ tablespoons butter, melted
- 1¼ tablespoons sugar
- ½ teaspoon salt
- acacia or millefiori honey

Preparation:

Mix the flour, baking powder, salt and sugar in a bowl.

Separate the eggs. Beat the whites to peaks and set aside. Beat the yolks and set aside.

In a bowl, combine the milk, egg yolks and melted butter.

Add the liquid ingredients to the dry ones, beating to form a smooth batter. Then add the egg whites beaten to peaks. Let stand for 30 minutes.

Melt butter in a fry pan, then add a ladle of the batter, letting it expand to cover the entire bottom.

Cook until the pancake darkens and small bubbles start to form, then turn and finish cooking on the other side.

Spread honey over each pancake and serve.

Soft bread with butter and Strawberry jam

Bread preparation time: 15 minutes - Total rising time: 1 hour and 40 minutes - Cooking time: 40 minutes
Jam preparation time: 30 minutes - Cooking time: 40–50 minutes

Ingredients for 1 loaf of bread:
- 4 cups all-purpose flour
- 1 cup water
- 1 tablespoon brewer's yeast
- 1 egg
- ⅓ cup butter, softened
- ¼ cup sugar
- 1 teaspoon salt

  For 3 medium jars:
- 6 ⅔ cups organic strawberries in season
- 1 ½ cups turbinado sugar or similar

Preparation:

Place the flour in a kneading machine. Add the egg and water, in which the yeast has previously been dissolved.

Knead until the flour has absorbed the ingredients, then add salt and sugar, and, little by little, the softened butter.

Place the dough in a bowl, cover with plastic wrap and let rise for approximately 60 minutes.

When the dough has doubled in size, knead lightly and place in a buttered bread pan.

Let it rise for a further 40 minutes, until the mixture reaches the edge of the pan.

Bake at 350°F for approximately 40 minutes.

Pane morbido, burro e confettura di fragole

Preparation
of jam:

Wash and halve the strawberies and place in a saucepan with a thick bottom. Add the sugar and place on a low heat.

Stir occasionally, making sure that the jam does not stick to the saucepan.

Cook for approximately 40 minutes – it will be ready when half a teaspoon of jam does not immediately expand if placed in a glass of cold water.

Pour the hot jam into jars. Close tightly, allow to cool and then refrigerate.

Eat within 1 month.

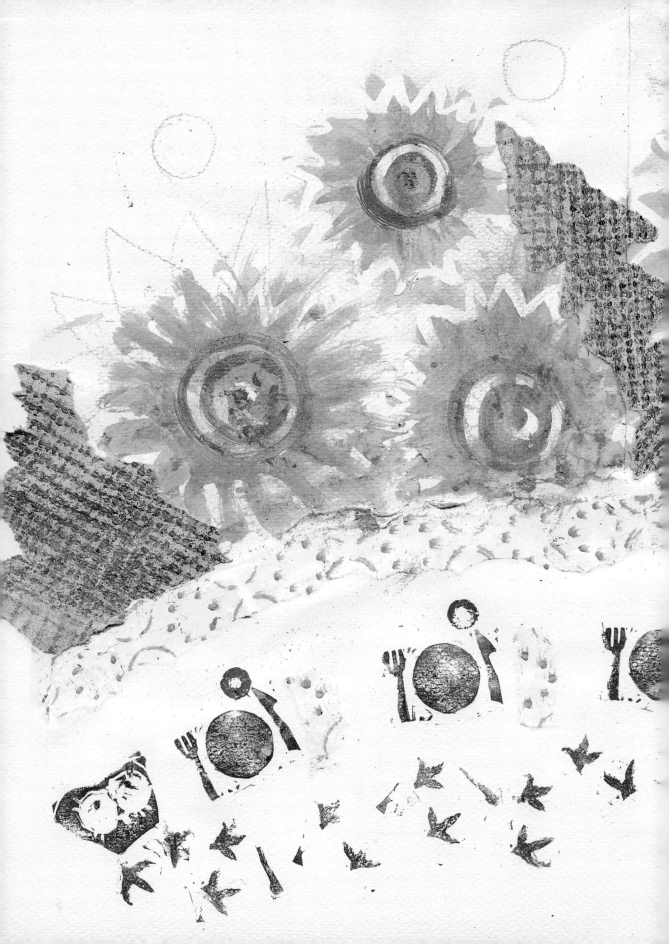

Omelette with ham, cheese and herbs

Preparation time: 20 minutes - Cooking time: 15 minutes

Ingredients:

- 2 eggs
- ¼ cup Gruyère cheese or similar, grated
- ¼ cup boiled ham (one piece), diced
- chives to taste
- Italian parsley to taste
- ¾ tablespoon butter
- 1 tablespoon extra virgin olive oil
- salt to taste
- pepper to taste

Tip:
The omelette should be eaten while still hot, possibly served with salad.

Preparation:

Break the eggs into a bowl and add the salt and pepper. Then using a fork, beat thoroughly but not for too long (the eggs should not incorporate too much air).

Finely chop the herbs.

Heat the oil and butter in a nonstick frying pan (preferably ceramic).

When the butter has melted, pour in the beaten eggs. When the edges of the omelette begin to set, use the fork to pull them towards the centre and tilt the pan so that the raw egg cooks.

When the center of the omelette is set, place the filling in the middle, lift the edges with a narrow spatula and fold in half.

Frittatina con prosciutto, formaggio e erbette

Spinach
pie

Preparation time: 30 minutes - Cooking time: 5 + 25 minutes

Ingredients for 6 people:

- 1 sheet puff pastry
- 1 lb fresh spinach leaves
- 1⅔ cups mixed melting cheeses, grated
- salt to taste
- pepper to taste

Crème royale sauce:
- ½ cup milk
- ½ cup fresh single cream
- 4 eggs

Preparation:

Boil the spinach in unsalted water for 5 minutes.

Line a round tart pan (9½" diameter with 1½" sides) with the pastry and refrigerate.

Mix the cheese with the well-drained spinach, season with salt and pepper, and pour the mixture into the tart pan.

Prepare the crème royale sauce by mixing the milk, cream and eggs.

Pour the sauce over the spinach and bake at 400°F for 25 minutes.

Serve warm.

Tortino con spinaci filanti

Bruschetta with tomatoes, olives and capers

Preparation time: 15 minutes - Cooking time: 5 minutes

Ingredients for 4 people:

- 4 slices crusty bread
- 2 ripe tomatoes
- 1 garlic clove
- 12 unsalted capers
- 8 pitted black olives
- a few basil leaves
- oregano to taste
- 2 tablespoons extra virgin olive oil
- salt to taste
- pepper to taste

Preparation:

Slit the tomatoes by making a cross on the bottom and plunge in boiling water for 40 seconds. Drain and place in iced water.

Peel and quarter, removing the seeds. Dice and place in a bowl. Add the capers, olives and chopped herbs. Season with salt and pepper, and add the oil.

Toast the bread on a barbecue or in the oven.

Lightly rub the garlic into the warm toast and then cover with the sauce.

Bruschettine con pomodori, olive e capperi

45

Hot chocolate

Preparation time: 10 minutes - Cooking time: 5 minutes

Ingredients for 6 cups:

- 2 cups chocolate, broken into pieces
- 4¼ cups cold full-cream milk
- 1 cup fresh cream from the refrigerator
- 1 vanilla pod
- 2 tablespoons cane sugar
- milk chocolate flakes to taste

Preparation:

Melt the chocolate pieces with ⅞ cup of milk over a low flame. Stir frequently to mix.

Cut the vanilla pod lengthwise and place it in a small saucepan with the remaining milk and the sugar. Bring to the boil.

Remove the vanilla pod and pass the milk through a fine strainer, then pour onto the melted chocolate and milk mixture.

Return to the stove for around 5 minutes, stirring with a whisk.

Whip the cream.

Pour the hot chocolate into cups. Add a teaspoon of the whipped cream and sprinkle with the milk chocolate flakes.

Cioccolata in tazza

46

Pizza
**Cheesy rice
balls**
French fries with
ketchup
The Frog Prince
Halloween ghosts

Pajama party

Pizza

Preparation time: 30 minutes - Rising time: 3 hours - Cooking time: 25 minutes

Ingredients for 1 pizza:

- 2 cups bread flour
- 1⅛ cups all-purpose flour
- 1 teaspoon brewer's yeast (1½ teaspoons in winter)
- 1 cup water
- ¼ cup extra virgin olive oil
- 2 teaspoons salt
- ⅔ cup cherry tomatoes, halved

Preparation:

Dissolve the yeast in the water, then mix the two types of flour with the water.

Incorporate 1½ tablespoons of the oil and, finally, the salt. Knead the dough until smooth.

Leave to rise for about 3 hours.

Roll out the dough into a circle with a rolling pin and sprinkle with salt and the remaining oil. Scatter the cherry tomatoes over the top.

Bake at 400°F for approoximately 25 minutes.

Pizza scrocchierella

Cheesy
rice balls

Preparation time: 30 minutes - Cooking time: 15 minutes
Frying time: 15 minutes - Resting time: 30 + 60 minutes

Ingredients for 20 rice balls:

- 1⅞ cups round grain rice
- 1¼ cups tomato purée
- 1 onion
- 5 cups vegetable stock
- 3 eggs
- 1¾ cups mozzarella
- ⅓ cup Parmesan cheese, grated
- 1⅔ cups breadcrumbs
- 1 large knob butter
- extra virgin olive oil
- peanut oil (for frying)
- salt to taste
- pepper to taste

Preparation of rice and tomato:

Make a liquid sauce using the onion, tomato purée and a drizzle of olive oil.

Add the rice to the sauce and cook over a fairly high flame, gradually adding the stock, until al dente. Season with salt and pepper, and remove from the heat. Add the butter and Parmesan, and stir.

Spread the rice on a baking sheet and allow to cool.

Preparation of rice balls:

Finely dice the mozzarella and place in a colander to drain off all the liquid.

When the rice is completely cool, take a tablespoon, add a few cubes of the mozzarella and carefully enclose it.

Dip into the beaten eggs and then in breadcrumbs.

Allow to stand for approximately 60 minutes, and then fry in ample hot oil (350°F). Place on kitchen paper to remove excess oil and serve hot.

French fries
with ketchup

Ketchup: preparation time: 30 minutes - Cooking time: 30 minutes
French fries: preparation time: 30 minutes - Cooking time: 20 minutes

Ingredients for 4 people:

French fries:
- 1 lb potatoes
- 6½ cups peanut oil or extra virgin
  olive oil for frying
- salt to taste

Ingredients for 1 cup ketchup:
- 2¾ cups San Marzano tomatoes,
  washed and chopped
- 1 sweet pepper
- 1 white onion
- 1 celery stick
- 1 carrot
- 1 garlic clove
- fresh herbs (sage, bay, chives,
  Italian parsley, basil, marjoram)
- 2 cloves
- ½ cinnamon stick
- 1 teaspoon coriander seeds
- 1 teaspoon cumin seeds
- 1 teaspoon mustard seeds
- 1 pinch nutmeg
- 1 teaspoon grated fresh ginger
- ½ cup extra virgin olive oil
- 2 tablespoons white wine
- vinegar
- 2 tablespoons superfine sugar
  salt to taste

Preparation of ketchup:

Crush and peel the garlic. Wash and
dry the pepper, and slice into strips,
removing the seeds and ribs. Clean
the celery. Peel the carrot and onion.
Chop all the ingredients and simmer
in a pan with a little oil, without
letting them brown.

Add the chopped tomatoes to the
pan. Sauté for 2–3 minutes, then add
all the herbs and spices. Cook over a
low heat for approximately
15 minutes, stirring occasionally.

Pass the sauce through a fine strainer
and transfer back to the frying pan
and cook until it thickens – around
10 minutes.

Once cooked, season with the sugar,
vinegar and salt.

Preparation of french fries:

Peel the potatoes and cut into evenly
sized fries. Place then in a bowl of
cold water.
After around 10 minutes, drain off all
the water and dry the potatoes in a
tea towel.

Heat the oil to approximately 335°F
and cook a few fries at a time.
Remove the excess oil with kitchen
paper and salt.

The Frog Prince

Rising time: 90 + 30 minutes - Cooking time: 25 minutes

Ingredients for 10 medium frogs:

- 10 cups all-purpose flour
- 1 tablespoon brewer's yeast
- 3 cups full-cream milk
- ½ cup softened butter
- 1 egg for glazing
- 20 raisins
- 2½ teaspoons sugar
- 2 teaspoons salt

Preparation:

Dissolve the yeast in the lukewarm milk.

In a kneading machine, knead the flour with the milk until fully absorbed, then add the sugar, the salt and, finally, the butter. Continue to knead until the dough is smooth and even.

Remove the dough from the machine and allow to rise in a large bowl covered with plastic wrap for 90 minutes.

Divide the dough into ten 5-oz pieces. Then divide each piece into a 3-oz ball and a 2-oz sausage.

By pressing gently, join the large ball (the body) to the sausage (the legs). Then firmly two raisins on the front of the body for eyes. Using a bottle top, make round indentations on the body. Using a sharp knife, form the mouth and feet.

Place on a baking sheet and leave to rise for a further 30 minutes.

Brush with the beaten egg and bake in a preheated oven at 400°F for 25 minutes.

Allow to cool and, if you like, make a crown for the frog using gold card.

Halloween ghosts

Preparation time: 20 minutes - Resting time: 30 minutes - Cooking time: 12/13 minutes

Ingredients for 30 ghosts:

- 6⅔ cups all-purpose flour
- 1½ cups butter, chilled
- 2 eggs
- 1 cup sugar

Icing:
- 2 cups confectioner's sugar
- 1¼ tablespoons egg whites
- 2 tablespoons lemon juice

Decoration:
- Black food decorating pen

Preparation:

Sift the flour and add the chopped butter, sugar and eggs. Quickly mix together, form the dough into a ball, cover with plastic wrap and refrigerate for 30 minutes.

Place the dough between 2 sheets of parchment paper and roll out to a thickness of ¼". Cut out the cookies using a floured ghost-shaped cutter.

Place on a baking sheet lined with wax paper and cook at 350°F for 12–13 minutes. Remove from the oven and allow to cool on a wire rack.

Sift the confectioner's sugar into a bowl, add the egg whites and lemon juice and whisk until smooth. Protect the icing with plastic wrap to avoid the surface setting.

Spoon the icing onto the cookies. Allow to dry and decorate with black food coloring.

I fantasmi di Halloween

Grandma and Grandpa drop by!

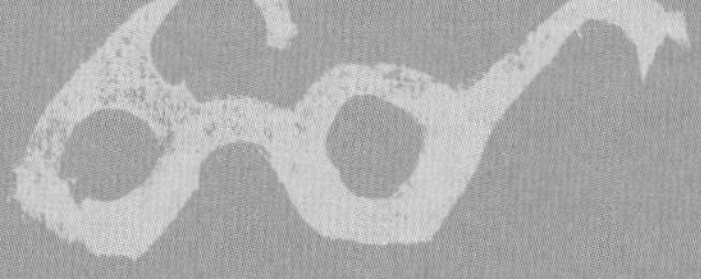

Spaghetti with
tomato and basil
**Risotto Milan
style**
Sautéed risotto
**Magic tomato
meatballs**
Saltimbocca
Roman style
**Upside-down
apple tart**
Carrot cake

Spaghetti with tomato and basil

Preparation time: 20 minutes - Cooking time: 10 minutes

Ingredients for 4 people:

- 12 oz spaghetti
- 2 lb ripe San Marzano tomatoes
- 2 garlic cloves
- a few basil leaves
- 4 tablespoons extra virgin olive oil
- salt to taste

Tip:
This is a classic Mediterranean dish. Although simple and quick to prepare, to get the best results you need to use sun-ripened tomatoes and good extra virgin olive oil. The dish doesn't need to be served with grated cheese.

Preparation:

Dip the tomatoes in boiling water for 15 seconds, then immerse in cold water. Peel, remove the seeds and cut into strips.

Heat the oil in a large frying pan and gently fry the 2 slightly crushed cloves of unpeeled garlic, making sure they don't darken. Once golden, remove the garlic and put the tomatoes in the frying pan. Raise the heat and cook for 10 minutes.

Cook the spaghetti in a large pan of boiling salted water.

Drain and add the spaghetti to the tomato sauce in the frying pan. Sauté for a few minutes, then add the fresh basil and serve.

Spaghetti al pomodoro e basilico

Risotto
Milan style

Preparation time: 10 minutes - Cooking time: 30 minutes

Ingredients for 4 people:

- 1⅔ cups Vialone Nano rice
- 1 tablespoon beef marrow
- ½ teaspoon saffron
- 1 shallot
- ¼ cup butter
- 6⅓ cups meat stock
- ⅓ cup grated Parmesan cheese
- 3 tablespoons extra virgin olive oil
- salt to taste

Tip:
If there are leftovers, use them the next day for a delicious Risotto al salto (see next recipe).

Preparation:

Fry the marrow and shallot in the olive oil, without browning, then set aside.

In a rice pan, heat the rice. When it feel quite hot to the touch, add the shallot and marrow.

After a few minutes, add the first ladle of hot stock, gradually adding the remainder, stirring constantly, until the rice is cooked – approximately 20 minutes.

Add the saffron, previously dissolved in a little of the stock.

Remove from the heat and thoroughly stir in the cold butter and Parmesan cheese to make the risotto creamy while still holding its shape.

Season with salt.

Risotto alla milanese

68

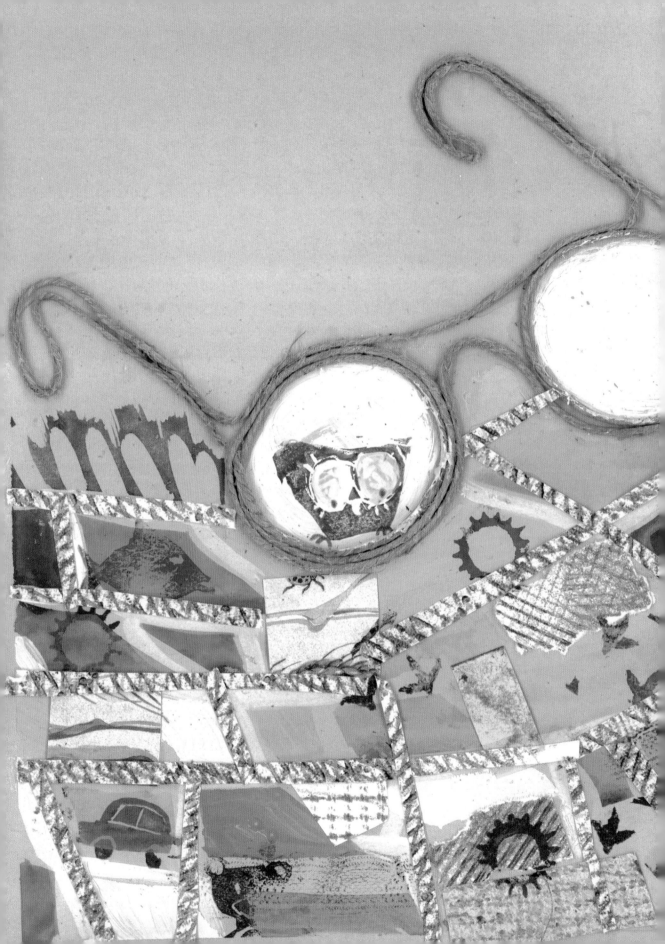

Sautéed risotto

Preparation time: 5 minutes - Cooking time: 10 minutes

Ingredients:
- cold risotto Milan style
- 1 small knob butter

Preparation:

Use a fork to slightly separate the grains and soften the leftover risotto.

Lightly butter a non-stick pan, add the risotto and squash it with the back of a spoon, dipped frequently in water. Cover the whole bottom of the pan to form a patty approximately ½" high.

Cook until a crust forms on both sides. Serve hot.

Risotto al salto

Magic tomato meatballs

Preparation time: 30 minutes - Cooking time: 30 minutes

Ingredients for 4 people:

- 1 cup ground beef
- 1 cup ground pork
- 3 cups peeled tomatoes, chopped
- ¼ lb good bread, crusts removed
- ½ cup grated Parmesan cheese
- 1 cup milk
- 1 egg
- 1 onion
- 1 garlic clove
- 1 handful chopped Italian parsley
- 5 tablespoons extra virgin olive oil
- salt to taste
- pepper to taste

Tip:
Meatball dishes have an infinite number of variations, depending on family traditions and the availability of ingredients. You can add sausage, two or three slices of mortadella or ham, or, according to the Neapolitan recipe, a couple of tablespoons of pine nuts and raisins. Garlic and parsley are traditional, but grated lemon zest, marjoram, nutmeg and finely chopped fresh spring onion all work well.

Preparation:

Soften the bread in the milk for 10 minutes, then thoroughly squeeze.

Mix the meat with the bread, then add the egg, Parmesan, parsley, and minced garlic. Season with salt and pepper. Combine carefully for a few minutes with your hands, until evenly mixed.

Divide into equal amounts and, after wetting your hands with a little oil, form balls about the size of a small egg, slightly flattened at the ends.

Finely chop the onion and fry well in 3 tablespoons of oil. Then add the chopped tomatoes and cook for 20 minutes.

In a non-stick pan quickly fry the meatballs in a little oil for 2 minutes on each side. Finally, transfer them to the sauce and cook for approximately 30 minutes.

Serve hot.

Magia di polpette al pomodoro

Saltimbocca
Roman style

Preparation time: 30 minutes - Cooking time: 15 minutes

Ingredients for 4 people:

- 12 veal escalopes (approximately 14 oz), trimmed and cut into small, thin slices (about the size of your palm)
- ¼ lb sweet prosciutto, sliced
- ½ cup white wine
- ample fresh sage in large leaves
- 1 knob of butter
- 2 tablespoons extra virgin olive oil
- flour as needed
- salt to taste
- pepper to taste

Preparation:

Line up the escalopes on a table, cover with plastic wrap and beat with a meat tenderizer.

Season with pepper and a little salt, and place a large sage leaf, washed and dried, on the middle of each.

Cover with a slice of prosciutto (the fat should not be removed) and secure the three layers with a toothpick.

Flour only the bottom part.

In a large frying pan, gently heat the oil and butter. Fry a few of the sage leaves, without allowing them to darken, and then place the saltimbocca in the pan, being careful that they do not overlap.

In a separate saucepan, remove the alcohol from the wine by boiling it for a few minutes over a high heat.

Cook the saltimbocca for 3–4 minutes at most on the floured side. When golden, pour the alcohol-free wine over the top.

As soon as the wine has evaporated, the saltimbocca are ready to be served with their sauce.

Saltimbocca
alla romana

SALta inBoCCA

AL
NONNO

Upside-down apple tart

Preparation time: 50 minutes - Resting time:: 30–60 minutes - Cooking time: 25 minutes

Ingredients for 8 people:

Pastry:
- 2½ cups all-purpose flour
- ½ cup chilled butter in small pieces
- 2 egg yolks
- 3-4 tablespoons cold water
- 1 pinch salt

Tart:
- 10 oz pastry
- 3½ lb golden delicious apples
- ⅔ cup butter
- ¾ cup sugar

Preparation of pastry:

In a bowl, rub the butter into the flour with your fingertips until the mixture resembles coarse breadcrumbs.

Make a well and add the egg yolks, and salt, using your whole hand to mix the ingredients together. Add water gradually as needed to form a smooth and even texture.

Shape the pastry into a ball, wrap in plastic wrap and refrigerate for 30–60 minutes.

Preparation of tart:

Roll out the pastry to form a disc the same size as a cake pan that can be placed on the stove. Turn the pan upside-down on the pastry and use a knife to remove excess pastry from around the edges. Place the pastry on parchment paper, prick with a fork and then refrigerate.

Peel, core and quarter the apples, then set aside.

Place the butter and sugar in the cake pan and cook on the stove until melted.

Arrange the apples in a circle in the pan. Return to the stove and cook for 40 minutes, checking the apples carefully and cooking only until the juice solidifies and turns golden. Remove from the heat and allow to cool.

Place the pastry disk, holes downward, over the apples, tucking in the edges.

Bake in preheated oven at 425°F for 25 minutes, until the pastry is golden. Remove from the oven and allow to cool slightly.

Turn the tart upside down onto a serving plate while still warm and before the caramel hardens, otherwise the job becomes difficult.

Crostata di mele al contrario

Carrot cake

Preparation time: 30 minutes - Cooking time: 55 minutes

Ingredients for one cake:

- 1⅞ cup all-purpose flour
- 1¾ cups carrots, chopped
- ¼ cup stewed apples
- ½ cup walnuts, shelled
- ¼ cup raisins
- 3 eggs
- ⅔ cup butter, melted
- 1 teaspoon baking powder
- 1 teaspoon baking soda
- 1 tsp ground cinnamon
- 1 cup superfine sugar
- pinch of salt

Preparation:

Preheat the oven to 350°F and place a baking sheet on the middle rack.

Soak the raisins in warm water. Squeeze the chopped carrots thorougly in a tea towel. Coarsely chop the walnuts.

In a large bowl, stir together the flour, baking soda, baking powder, cinnamon and salt.

In another bowl, beat the eggs, adding sugar to obtain a foamy consistency.

Slowly pour the warm melted butter into the eggs, add the stewed apples, and pour the mixture into the flour. Stir with a spatula and, when half mixed, add the carrots, squeezed draisins and walnuts. Continue to stir until an even texture.

Pour the batter into a buttered and lightly floured loaf pan. To prevent the formation of air bubbles, tap it on a table.

Place the pan in the oven on a baking sheet and bake for 55 minutes.

When the cake is cooked (pierce with a toothpick to check), run a knife around the edge of the pan.

Allow to stand for 15 minutes before removing from the pan, then let it cool on a cake rack.

Dolce alle carote

Chocolate buns
Squirrel bread
**Flatbread the
way I like it**
Creamy muesli
with fresh and
dried fruit
**Wild strawberry
and honey
smoothie**
Berry and
peppermint fruit
salad

Friends over
to do homework

Chocolate buns

Rising time: 1 hours 40 minutes - Cooking time: 10–15 minutes

Ingredients for approximately 20 buns:
- 3½ cups all-purpose flour
- 3½ cups bread flour
- ½ cup dark or milk chocolate chips
- ⅓ cup acacia or wildflower honey
- ½ cup butter, softened
- 2 whole eggs and 4 egg yolks
- 1 tablespoon brewer's yeast
- milk as needed
- ⅞ cup water
- 2½ teaspoons salt

Preparation:

Dissolve the yeast in water.

Gently beat the eggs together with the honey and add to the water.

Add the liquid to the two types of flour in a kneading machine.

Once the dough is smooth, add the softened butter and, finally, the salt and chocolate.

Let the mixture rise in a large bowl covered with plastic wrap until doubled in size – approximately 60 minutes.

Divide the dough into approximately 1 oz portions. Form into balls and arrange on a baking sheet with a non-stick surface or lined with parchment paper.

Allow to rise further, until the balls have doubled in size – approximately 40 minutes.

Brush the buns with the egg yolks combined with the milk.

Bake at 180°C for 10–15 minutes.

Squirrel
bread

Preparation time: 15 minutes

Ingredients for 4 people:

- 4 slices sliced wholemeal bread
- 4 tablespoons honey
- 4 walnuts
- 4 hazelnuts
- 4 squares milk chocolate

Preparation:

Toast the bread or grill in the oven for 1 minute.

Spread each slice with honey and set aside.

Coarsely chop the walnuts, hazelnuts and chocolate.

Cover each slice with the chopped nuts and chocolate.

Pane integrale
degli scoiattoli

Flatbread
the way I like it

Preparation time: 20 minutes - Resting time: 30 minutes - Cooking time: 6 minutes

Ingredients for 7 flatbreads:

- 2 cups all-purpose flour
- ½ cup lard
- ¾ teaspoon baking powder
- ¾ teaspoon baking soda
- ¼ cup cold sparkling water
- ½ cup milk
- 1 tablespoon salt

Tip:
Possible fillings for the flatbreads include sliced ham, arugula and ⅝ cup soft cheese; sliced mortadella, sliced salami and a few lettuce leaves; 2 tomatoes and tuna in brine. Or you can eat them sweet, spread with hazelnut cream.

Preparation:

Place the flour and salt in a kneading machine. Add the lard, water, milk, baking soda and baking powder.

Knead at medium speed at first, then finish at high speed.

Wrap the dough in plastic wrap and refrigerate for 30 minutes.

Roll out the dough with a rolling pin and cut into discs.

Cook the flatbreads for 3 minutes each side in a small frying pan on an iron or terracotta griddle. If the griddle becomes too warm, turn off the heat for a few minutes.

Serve hot topped with whatever you like.

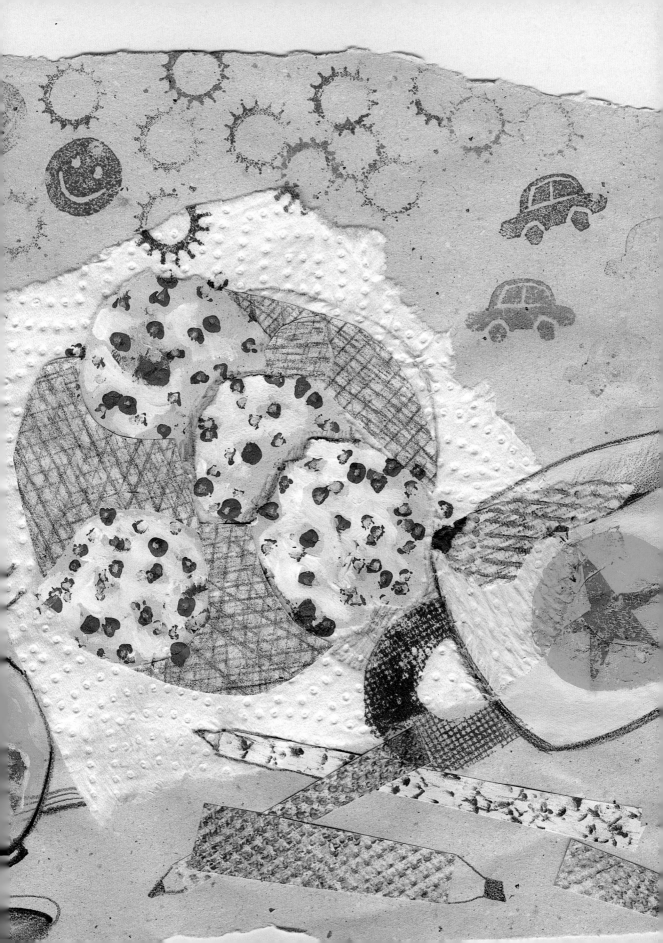

Creamy muesli
with fresh and dried fruit

Preparation time: 15 minutes

Ingredients for 4 small bowls:
- ⅓ cup rolled oats
- ⅓ cup rolled barley flakes
- ⅓ cup raisins
- ¼ cup organic dried apricots
- ⅛ cup organic dried pineapple
- 1 banana
- 1 appe
- 1¼ cup unsweetened plain yogurt
- 2 tablespoons barley or rice malt

Preparation:

In a large container, mix the rolled oats, barley flakes, raisins, diced apricots and pineapple.

Peel and cube the apples – to stop them from turning brown, dip them in a bowl of sparkling water. Add the well-drained diced apple to the other ingredients.

Pour on the yogurt. Only at this point, peel the banana, slice and add to the rest of the ingredients.

Mix gently and add the malt to sweeten.

Muesli cremoso con frutta fresca e secca

Wild strawberry
and honey smoothie

Preparation time: 15 minutes

Ingredients for 6 glasses:

- 4¼ cups very cold fresh milk
- 2½ cups wild strawberries
- 2 tablespoons acacia or millefiori
  honey

Preparation:

Blend the strawberries with the milk
and honey.

Filter through a fine strainer and
serve.

Frullato di fragoline di bosco e miele

Berry and peppermint fruit salad

Preparation time: 30 minutes - Cooking time: 15 minutes - Resting time: 20 minutes

Ingredients for 4 small bowls:

- 1 cup blackcurrants
- ⅞ cup + 2 cups raspberries
- 3⅓ cups strawberries
- ⅞ cup blackberries
- ⅞ cup blueberries
- 1 bunch fresh peppermint
- 1¼ cups water
- ¾ cup superfine sugar

Preparation:

In a saucepan, bring the water, sugar, blackcurrants and ⅞ cup of raspberries to the boil.

Remove from the heat and add the peppermint leaves. Allow to steep for 20 minutes before removing the peppermint.

Using a hand blender, blend everything, then strain the syrup through a fine sieve. Store in a cool place.

Quarter the strawberries and add to the other fresh fruit.

Put a ladle of syrup into each bowl, then add the fresh fruit.

Macedonia di fruttini e menta piperita

Vegetable soup with crispy fish balls

Chicken and spinach nuggets with light mashed potato

Fish fingers

Rainbow salad with tuna

Help! Exams!

Vegetable soup with crispy fish balls

Vegetable soup: preparation time: 30 minutes - Cooking time: 2 hours
Fish balls: preparation time 30 minutes - Cooking time: 40 minutes

Ingredients for 4 people:

Vegetable soup:
- 2 medium potatoes
- 2 zucchini
- 3 carrots
- 1 rib celery
- ½ cup Savoy cabbage, shredded
- 1 cup fresh borlotti or cannellini beans
- 4 peeled tomatoes
- 1 large brown onion
- 1 garlic clove
- 8½ cups vegetable stock (celery, carrot and onion)
- 3 tablespoons extra virgin olive oil
- salt to taste

Fish balls:
- 1¼ cups leftover fish (grouper, dentex, sea bass, hake and/or salt or fresh cod)
- 1 lb 2oz floury old potatoes
- 2 eggs
- 1¼ cups breadcrumbs
- 1 handful flour
- 1 handful Italian parsley
- salt to taste
- pepper to taste
- extra virgin olive oil
- peanut oil for frying

Preparation of vegetable soup:

In a saucepan, fry the unpeeled clove of garlic, removing it when it has browned.

Add the finely chopped onion and carrots, the trimmed and diced celery, the shredded cabbage, the tomatoes and beans.

Turn up the heat and, stirring continuously, fry the vegetables for about 10 minutes. Now add the boiling stock.

Wash and peel the potatoes, and add them whole to the soup.

Cover the pan and cook for at least 90 minutes. At this point, add the diced zucchini and cook for a further 30 minutes.

Once cooked, blend with a hand blender and keep warm.

Passato di verdure
con polpettine croccanti di pesce

Preparation
of fish balls:

Wash the potatoes without peeling them, place in cold water and boil. When cooked, peel and mash them.

Meanwhile, break the fish up with a fork, taking care to remove all the bones and skin.

Mix the same amounts of potato and fish with finely chopped parsley, season with salt and pepper, and continue to knead by hand until the mixture is an even texture.

With your hands lightly floured, form balls of the mixture about the size of a cherry. One by one, flour the balls, dip into the beaten eggs, and roll in the breadcrumbs.

Pour plenty of oil into a wok (the fish balls must be able to float) and when hot (350°F) fry a few at a time for 3–4 minutes.

Drain, place on a double sheet of kitchen paper to remove excess oil, and keep warm.

Place 2 ladles of the soup in a deep bowl and arrange 4 fish balls in the middle. Garnish with chopped parsley and a drizzle of olive oil.

Chicken and spinach
nuggets with light mashed potato

Nuggets: preparation time: 30 minutes - Cooking time: 20 minutes
Mashed potato: preparation time: 10 minutes - Cooking time: 40 minutes

Ingredients for 4 people:

Nuggets:
- ¾ lb raw chicken meat
- 1 lb fresh spinach leaves
- ⅞ cup sheep's milk ricotta cheese
- 2 whole eggs and 1 yolk
- 2 tablespoons flour
- 2 handfuls breadcrumbs
- grated zest of ½ lemon
- extra virgin olive oil or peanut oil
  for frying
- salt to taste
- pepper to taste

Mashed potato:
- 2¼ lb potatoes (yellow if possible)
- juice of 1 lemon
- extra virgin olive oil
- salt to taste

Preparation
of nuggets:

Boil and bone the chicken, removing
all skin and cartilage. Mince the
chicken for a few seconds, stopping
before it turns to a purée.

Boil the spinach in plenty of boiling
water. Drain, squeeze out the water
in a tea cloth, chop and set aside.

Place the chicken in a bowl with the
ricotta, spinach and the lemon zest,
and add salt and pepper.

Knead the mixture with your hands
until completely mixed, then divide
it into portions about the size of an
apricot.

Grease your hands with a little oil
and form small balls.

Lightly flour the nuggets, dip in the
beaten eggs and then coat thoroughly
with breadcrumbs.

Fry the nuggets in hot oil in a frying
pan for a few minutes on each side.

When golden brown, drain and place
on a double sheet of kitchen paper to
remove excess oil. Keep warm. (But
they're also good cold.)

Preparation of the mashed potato:

Wash the potatoes without peeling them. Dry them and wrap in aluminium foil with the dull side on the outside.

Make a hole in the foil with a knife and arrange the potatoes hole side down on a baking sheet covered with coarse salt.

Roast at 300°F for approximately 40 minutes.

Remove the potatoes from the oven and discard the foil. Peel and mash.

Add the oil and beat the mashed potato with a wooden spoon in a saucepan. At the very end, add the strained lemon juice and salt. Serve with the nuggets.

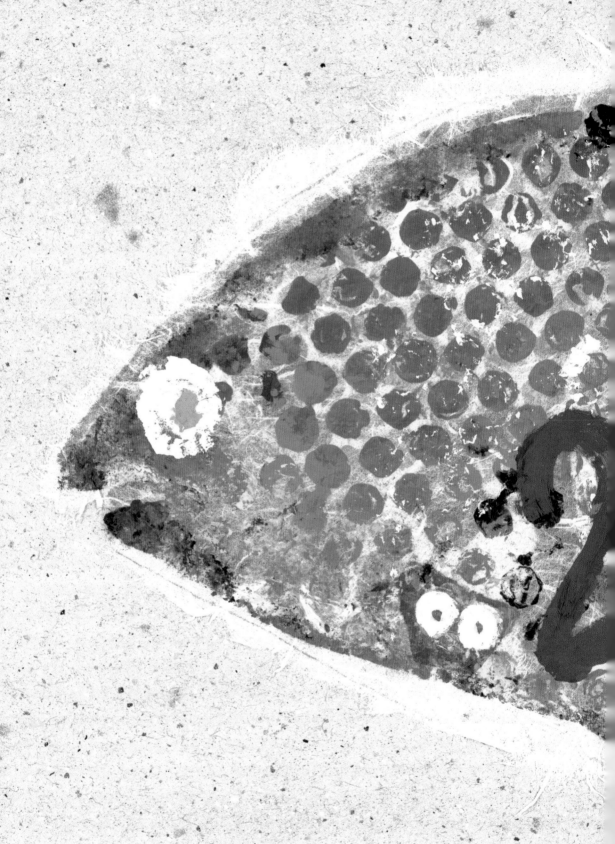

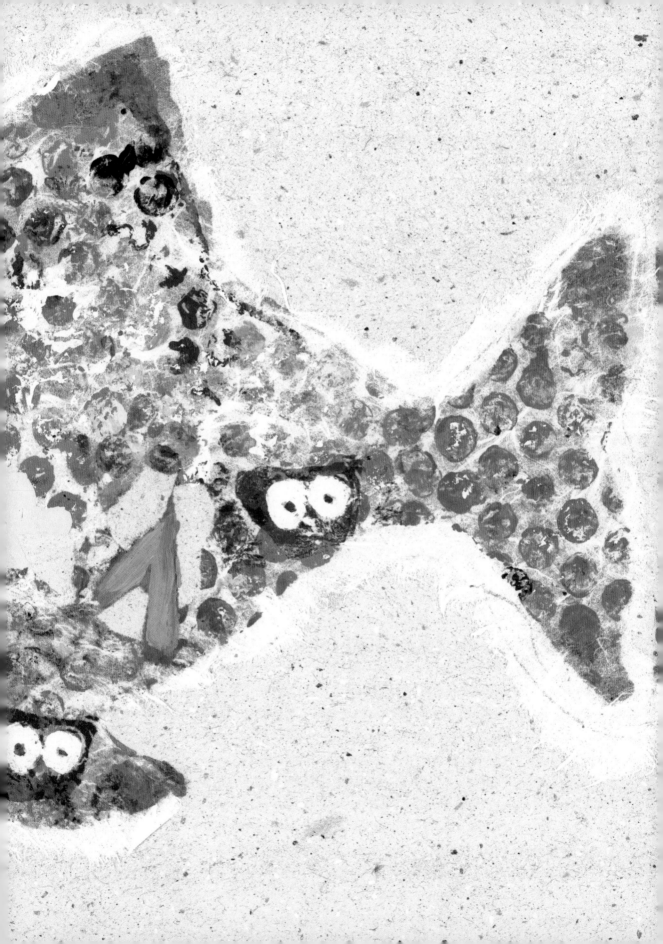

Fish fingers

Preparation time: 20 minutes - Cooking time: 10 minutes

Ingredients for 4 people:

- 8 sole or flounder fillets
- 3 eggs
- 1 tablespoon fresh chives
- grated zest of 1 organic lemon
- 6 tablespoons breadcrumbs
- 4 tablespoons extra virgin olive oil
- salt to taste
- pepper to taste

Preparazione:

Lie each fillet between two sheets of plastic wrap and beat lightly with a meat tenderizer.

Remove the plastic wrap, take 2 fillets and place one on top of the other. Fold them to make sticks. Compress them using the wrap, first forming rolls and then flattening them. Set aside.

Beat the eggs in a bowl and add salt and pepper to taste. Mix together the breadcrumbs, chives and lemon zest in a wide bowl.

Remove the plastic wrap from the fish fingers and pat them dry with kitchen paper. Gently dip them in beaten egg and then in the breadcrumbs, ensuring that they are well coated.

Heat the oil in a frying pan and cook the fish fingers for about 3 minutes on each side, until golden.

Remove with a fish slice and place on a double sheet of kitchen paper to absorb excess oil.

Bastoncini di pesce

SOLE

Rainbow salad
with tuna

Preparation time: 20 minutes - Cooking time: 10 minutes

Ingredients for 4 people:

- 10½ oz fine green beans
- 7 oz small zucchini
- 1 yellow pepper
- 10½ oz ripe tomatoes
- 1 cup canned tuna in brine
- fresh basil
- fresh oregano
- 2 tablespoons extra virgin olive oil
- salt to taste
- pepper to taste

Preparation:

Trim and wash the beans. Wash and dice the zucchini.

Blanch the beans for 5 minutes, then plunge immediately into iced water to preserve their color. Repeat with the zucchini.

Wash the tomatoes and slice horizontally. Wash the pepper and carefully remove the stalk, seeds and white ribs. Cut into quarters and then into strips.

Arrange the cooked and raw vegetables attractively in a salad bowl. Place the flaked tuna in the center. Sprinkle with the basil and oregano, and season with the oil, salt and pepper.

Insalata arcobaleno con tonno

A tribute to my friend Rania

Couscous with chickpeas and vegetables and gingered chicken
Meat-stuffed crescents
Bulgur with fish and vegetables
Rice pudding with raisins
Yoghurt cake with pineapple and kiwi fruit
Hibiscus tea
Lemon sherbet

Couscous with chickpeas and vegetables and gingered chicken

Preparation time: 30 minutes - Cooking time: 50 minutes

Ingredients for 4 people:

- 1¾ cups precooked couscous (medium grain)
- 1 lb chicken breast, chopped
- 1 cup dried chickpeas
- 3 carrots, peeled
- 2 zucchini
- 2 white onions, peeled
- 1 teaspoon turmeric
- 1 bunch fresh cilantro
- 1 fresh ginger root (medium sized)
- ⅓ cup canned chopped tomatoes
- 2¼ cups vegetable stock (celery, carrot and onion)
- 6 tablespoons extra virgin olive oil
- salt to taste
- pepper to taste

Preparation:

Soak the chickpeas overnight.

The following day, cook them for about 30 minutes in plenty of water.

Place the couscous in a bowl, add 2 cups hot vegetable stock, cover with a tea towel and wait until all the stock has been absorbed.

Heat the oil in a large saucepan and lightly sauté the onions, cut into thin segments, then add the thickly sliced carrots and the diced zucchini. Add the meat, cut into chunks the size of a walnut. Season with salt and pepper to taste.

Peel the ginger root, grate it and squeeze the flesh. Pass the juice through a fine strainer and set aside.

Drain the chickpeas and add to the pan, together with the turmeric, chopped cilantro and tomatoes.

Couscous con ceci e verdure e pollo allo zenzero

When the meat and vegetables are
tender, add the ginger juice a little at
a time, tasting to ensure that the dish
is not excessively spicy.

Lower the heat and allow to simmer
gently for about 20 minutes, adding
the remaining stock.

Place the couscous and the stew in
a tajine (or other terracotta dish) and
serve.

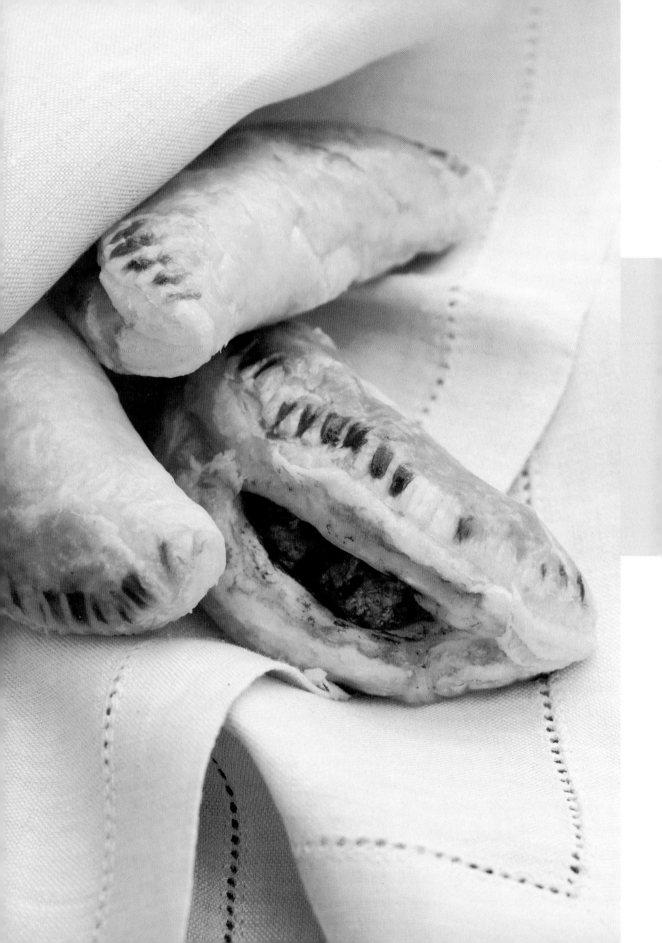

Meat-stuffed crescents

Preparation time: 30 minutes - Cooking time: 40 minutes

Ingredients for 4 people:

- 1⅔ cups ground beef
- 1 lb puff pastry
- 8 cherry tomatoes
- 2 spring onions
- 1 garlic clove
- 1 teaspoon ground cumin
- 1 teaspoon ground coriander
- 1 teaspoon ground cinnamon
- 2 tablespoons chopped Italian parsley
- 1 egg yolk
- 2 tablespoons milk
- extra virgin olive oil
- salt to taste
- pepper to taste

Preparation:

Heat the oil in a frying pan and sauté the lightly crushed clove of garlic until golden. Remove the garlic and lightly sauté the finely chopped spring onions. Add the meat and the spices and continue cooking for 10 minutes. Season to taste with salt and pepper.

Cut out 10 discs of pastry, each 4" in diameter.

Wash and dice the tomatoes and add them to the meat together with the parsley.

Leave to cool before dividing between the pastry discs. Fold each one over, press firmly to seal and shape into crescents.

Arrange the crescents on a baking sheet lined with parchment paper. Brush with the egg yolk beaten with the milk.

Bake at 400°F for 20 minutes.

Mezzelune ripiene di carne

Bulgur with fish and vegetables

Preparation time: 30 minutes - Cooking time: 60 minutes

Ingredients for 4 people:

- 1¾ cups fine-ground bulgur
- 1½ lb non-bony fish (cod, plaice, oily fish)
- 1 white onion
- 3 carrots
- 3 white turnips
- 2 quinces
- saffron strands to taste
- ½ teaspoon fresh thyme
- 2¼ cups vegetable stock (celery, carrot and onion)
- 2¼ cups fish stock (head and tails)
- 5 tablespoons extra virgin olive oil
- salt to taste

Preparation:

Peel and chop the onion. Wash, trim and dice all the vegetables.

Heat the oil in a frying pan and sauté the vegetables. When they are golden, add the bulgur, cook for a few more minutes and then add the vegetable stock and the saffron strands dissolved in a ladle of stock.

Cover the pan and cook over a low heat for 20 minutes. Season with salt.

Peel, core and slice the quinces and poach them together with the fish for 20 minutes in the fish stock.

Place the bulgur and vegetables in a tajine (or other terracotta dish) and top with the fish and the quinces. Sprinkle with fresh thyme and serve.

Burghul con pesce e verdure

Rice pudding
with raisins

Preparation time: 20 minutes - Cooking time: 25 minutes - Refrigeration time: 30 minutes

Ingredients for 6 people:

- 1 cup Arborio rice
- 1½ cups full-cream milk
- 1 vanilla pod
- ⅜ cup raisins
- ⅔ cup superfine sugar
- ground cinnamon to taste

Tip:
Allow the puddings to cool before serving and accompany them with caramelized fruit of your choice.

Preparation:

Boil the rice and drain it while still al dente.

Score the vanilla pod lengthwise and add to a saucepan with the milk and sugar.

When the mixture starts to boil, add the rice and allow to cook for 15 minutes until all the liquid has been absorbed.

Soak the raisins in hot water for a few minutes to soften, then squeeze out the liquid and add them to the mixture.

Fill individual silicone molds with the rice and refrigerate for at least 30 minutes until set.

Unmold the rice puddings and sprinkle with the ground cinnamon.

Budino di riso e uvetta

Yoghurt cake
with pineapple and kiwi fruit

Preparation time: 30 minutes - Cooking time: 40 minutes

Ingredients for 6 portions:

- 3 cups soft wheat semolina
- ⅔ cup unsweetened plain yogurt
- 1 cup ground almonds
- 3 eggs
- 1½ cups superfine sugar
- 1⅓ cups confectioner's sugar
- ½ cup softened butter
- juice and grated zest of 1 organic orange
- 2½ teaspoons baking powder
- 5 slices pineapple
- 2 kiwi fruit

Preparation:

Cream the butter with the confectioner's sugar, orange zest and eggs until smooth and fluffy.

Sift the semolina and baking powder into the mixture.

Stir the ground almonds into the yoghurt and add to the mixture.

Transfer the batter to a greased 10"-diameter springform pan tin and bake in a preheated oven at 350°F for 40 minutes.

Turn out and allow to cool on a wire rack.

In the meantime, bring 1 cup water to boil with the superfine sugar and the orange juice. Heat to 185°F and allow the syrup to cool.

Pierce the cake with a skewer and pour the syrup over it.

Dredge with confectioner's sugar before serving, accompanying each slice with the diced pineapple and kiwi fruit.

Cover the cake if not serving immediately.

Hibiscus tea

Preparation time: 5 minutes - Cooking time: 10 minutes - Infusion time: 20 minutes

Ingredients for one 50-oz pitcher:

- 3 tablespoons dried hibiscus flowers
- 4 fresh mint leaves
- 4 fresh lemon balm leaves
- juice of 1 lemon
- acacia honey or turbinado sugar to taste

Tip:
This particularly refreshing, thirst-quenching drink can be served hot or cold and is also good unsweetened.

Preparation:

Bring the water to the boil, add the hibiscus flowers and remove from the heat. Add the mint and lemon balm leaves. Cover and infuse for 20 minutes.

Filter the drink through a fine strainer. Pour into the pitcher and add the strained lemon juice.

Sweeten with acacia honey or turbinado sugar if wished.

Karkadè

130

Lemon sherbet

Preparation time: 10 minutes - Cooking time: 20 minutes - Resting time: overnight

Ingredients for one 50-oz pitcher:

- ⅔ cup lemon juice, strained
- ¾ cup superfine sugar
- grated zest of 1 organic lemon
- grated zest of 1 organic orange
- 10 mint leaves
- 4¼ cups sparkling mineral water
- ice cubes

Preparation:

Bring the lemon juice to the boil with the sugar and the orange and lemon zest.

Add the washed mint leaves and boil for a further 10 minutes.

Strain the juice, pour into a pitcher and cover with plastic wrap. Allow to cool and then refrigerate overnight.

To serve, place a tablespoon of syrup in a glass and fill with sparkling water and ice cubes.

Sherbet al limone

Risotto with crispy
artichokes
**Cheesy Easter
bread**
White asparagus
with eggs

Easter

Risotto with crispy artichokes

Preparation time: 20 minutes - Cooking time 25 minutes

Ingredients for 4 people:

- 1⅔ cups Vialone Nano or Carnaroli rice
- 4 baby artichokes
- 1 garlic clove
- 2 shallots
- 4¼ cups vegetable stock (celery, carrot and onion)
- ¼ cup white wine
- juice of ½ lemon
- a few mint leaves
- 2 tablespoons grated Parmesan cheese
- 2 tablespoons grated Pecorino cheese
- 2 tablespoons butter, chilled
- 3 tablespoons extra virgin olive oil
- salt to taste
- pepper to taste

Preparation:

Use the hearts of the artichokes only. Slice as thinly as possible and drop into a bowl of water and lemon juice.

Heat the oil in a frying pan and sauté the slightly crushed unpeeled clove of garlic, then add the drained artichoke slices, a few at a time. Cook for a few minutes until golden, flavor with the mint and keep warm.

Remove the alcohol from the wine by allowing it to simmer for a few minutes, then set aside. Sauté the shallots in the olive oil and set aside.

In a rice pan, preferably copper, heat the dry rice. When it is too hot to touch, add the alcohol-free wine and then the shallot.

After a few minutes, add a ladle of boiling stock, stirring constantly. Gradually add the remaining stock until the rice is cooked – approximately 20 minutes.

Remove from the heat, add the cheese and the butter, cut into dice, beat well until creamy, and add the crispy artichokes. Season with salt and pepper to taste.

Cheesy Easter bread

Preparation time: 40 minutes - Rising time: 2 hours - Cooking time: 55 minutes

Ingredients for one 8"-diameter loaf:

- 5 cups all-purpose flour
- 5 eggs
- 2½ tablespoons brewer's yeast
- ½ cup Parmesan cheese, grated
- ½ cup Pecorino Romano cheese, grated
- ½ cup Gruyère cheese or similar, grated
- ⅔ cup butter (or lard and butter)
- 2 teaspoons salt
- pepper to taste
- ⅔ cup water

Tip:
Easter bread is excellent with Pecorino cheese and fresh fava beans.

Preparation:

Grind the pepper into the water in a small saucepan and bring to the boil.

Heat the eggs and butter with the water and pepper in a bain-marie. Ensure that the temperature does not reach 180°F to avoid curdling the eggs.

Add the cheeses and salt to taste.

Add the flour and the yeast to form a dough and mix in a kneading machine until smooth.

Place the dough in a deep round pan and leave to rise for 2 hours until it reaches the edges of the pan.

Place the bread in an oven preheated to 400°F, reduce the temperature to 350°F and bake for approximately 55 minutes.

Pane di Pasqua al formaggio

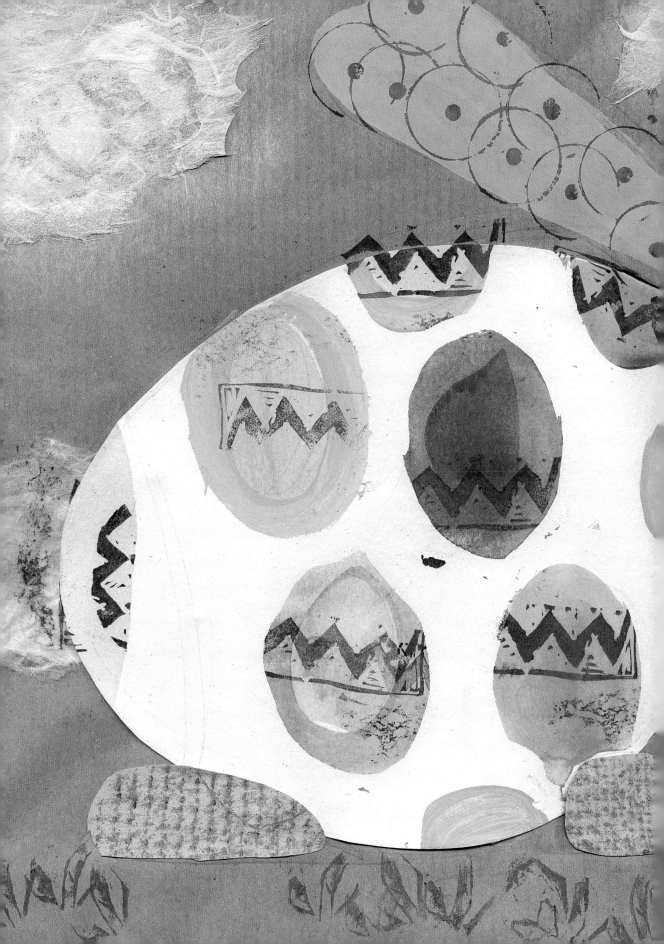

White asparagus with eggs

Preparation time: 15 minutes - Cooking time: 20 + 10 minutes

Ingredients for 4 people:

- 24 spears white asparagus
- 6 eggs
- extra virgin olive oil to taste
- vinegar to taste
- salt to taste

Preparation:

Peel the spears of asparagus with a potato peeler and cook them upright in a steamer or in a saucepan half full of water.

In the meantime, hard boil the eggs by bringing them to the boil in a pan of cold water then cooking for 10 minutes. Cool them under cold running water and shell.

Serve the asparagus with the hard-boiled eggs cut into segments or mashed with a fork.

Season with a drizzle of olive oil, salt and vinegar to taste.

Asparagi bianchi con le uova

147

Spring picnic

Fusilli pasta salad with tuna and tomato

Pennette pasta salad with mozzarella, tomatoes, pine nuts and anchovies

Tuna, cheese and arugula filled bread

Crudités

Focaccia with crispy prosciutto

Uncle Gufo's chicken salad

Cherry volcano

Fusilli pasta salad with tuna and tomato

Preparation time: 15 minutes - Cooking time: 10 minutes

Ingredients for 4 people:

- 2½ cups fusilli pasta
- 1 cup canned tuna fillet in oil
- 2 large tomatoes
- 1 bunch mixed salad leaves (radicchio, romaine lettuce, iceberg lettuce)
- 1 teaspoon fresh oregano
- 2 tablespoons extra virgin olive oil
- salt to taste

Preparation:

Cook the pasta in a large pan of boiling salted water, drain when al dente and cool under cold running water.

Wash the salad leaves and dry on kitchen paper. Tear into pieces with your hands.

Wash the tomatoes and cut into thin segments.

Place the pasta, salad leaves and tomatoes in a large salad bowl, sprinkle with oregano and arrange the flaked tuna in the center.

Drizzle over the olive oil before serving.

Insalata di fusilli con tonno e pomodoro

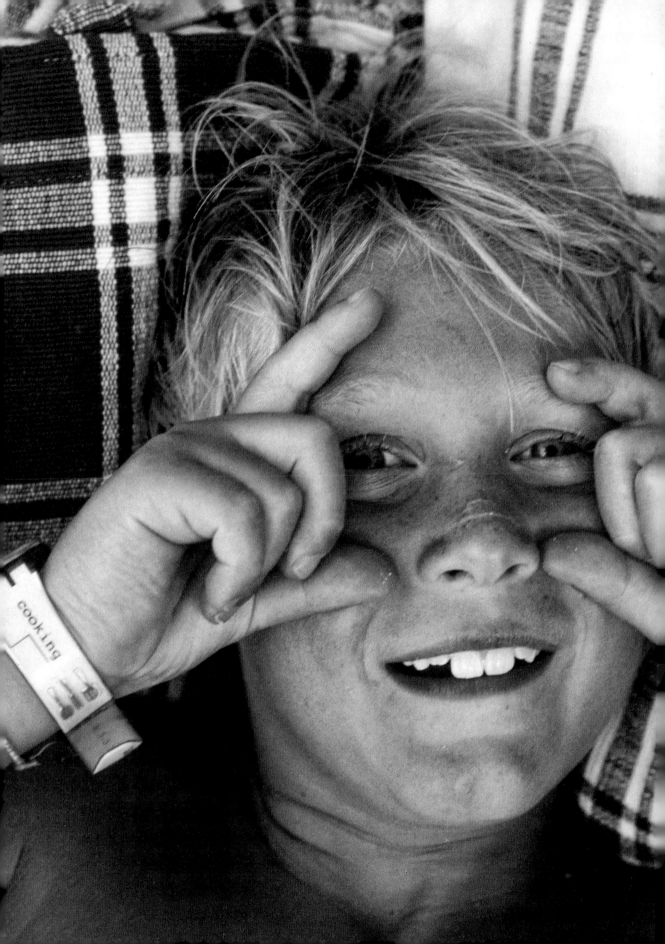

Pennette pasta salad with mozzarella, tomatoes, pine nuts and anchovies

Preparation time: 20 minutes - Cooking time: 15 minutes

Ingredients for 4 people:

- 3 cups pennette pasta
- 2 ripe tomatoes
- 2¼ cups mozzarella, diced
- 1 tablespoon pine nuts
- 4 anchovy fillets in oil
- 2 tablespoons extra virgin olive oil
- salt to taste

Preparation:

Cook the pasta in a large pan of boiling salted water, drain when al dente and cool under cold running water. Set aside.

Make an incision on the bottom of the tomatoes and plunge them into boiling water for a few seconds. Cool them in a bowl of cold water, then peel and deseed them before dicing.

Place the diced mozzarella in a colander to drain off all the liquid.

In a large bowl, toss the pasta with the tomatoes, mozzarella, pine nuts and chopped anchovy fillets and serve.

Insalata di
pennette con
mozzarella,
pomodori, pinoli
e acciughe

Tuna, cheese and arugula filled bread

Preparation time: 20 minutes - Resting time: 30 minutes

Ingredients for 4 people:

- 2 baguettes
- 1 thick slice boiled ham (approx. 3½ oz)
- 1¾ cups canned tuna steaks in brine
- ½ cup soft goat's cheese
- ⅔ cup softened butter
- 1 bunch arugula
- salt to taste

Preparation:

Dice the ham and whizz in a blender with the goat's cheese and tuna for a few seconds at medium speed.

Finely chop the arugula, stopping before it becomes a purée.

In a large bowl, beat the ham and cheese mixture with the remaining ingredients (including the butter).

Season with salt.

Cut each baguette into two pieces and hollow them out.

Stuff with the filling, using a pastry bag.

Cover with plastic wrap and refrigerate for 30 minutes.

Cut each piece into 4 slices and serve.

Pane ripieno di tonno, formaggio e rucola

Crudités

Preparation time: 30 minutes

Ingredients for 4 people:

- 2 sweet peppers
- 4 carrots
- 2 ribs white celery
- chives, finely chopped
- juice of 1 lemon
- 1 carton thick yogurt
- 1 tablespoon sweet mustard
- 6 tablespoons extra virgin olive oil
- salt to taste
- pepper to taste

Preparation:

Cut all the vegetables into sticks and set aside.

In a small bowl, beat together the oil, strained lemon juice, chives, and salt and pepper with a fork.

In another bowl, mix the yogurt with a tablespoon of oil and the mustard.

Serve the vegetables with the sauces.

Pinzimonio

Focaccia
with crispy prosciutto

Preparation time: 30 minutes - Total rising time: 2 hours 40 minutes - Cooking time: 45 minutes

Ingredients for 1 focaccia:

- 7 cups all-purpose flour
- 7 oz prosciutto (one piece)
- ½ cup wheat germ
- 2½ teaspoons rice malt or barley malt
- ¾ tablespoon brewer's yeast
- 1⅓ cups water
- 2½ tablespoons extra virgin olive oil
- 3 teaspoons coarse salt

Ingredients for brine:
- 2 tablespoons water
- 1⅔ tablespoons extra virgin olive oil
- 3 teaspoons coarse salt

Preparation:

Cut the prosciutto into thin strips and sauté in a pan without oil. Set aside.

Dissolve the yeast in the water.

Add the flour and wheat germ to the kneading machine, along with the water and the malt. Allow the flour to absorb the water before starting to knead. Add the salt and, finally, the oil.

When the dough has absorbed the oil, add the prosciutto and knead for a few more minutes.

Transfer the dough to a large bowl and cover with plastic wrap. Allow to rise for a couple of hours until doubled in size.

Press the dough out onto a lightly oiled baking sheet and allow to rise again for approximately 40 minutes.

Prepare the brine by mixing the water, oil and salt. Sprinkle it over the focaccia and bake at 400°F for about 45 minutes.

Remove from the oven and the baking sheet and allow to cool on a wire rack before cutting.

Uncle Gufo's chicken salad

Preparation time: 30 minutes - Cooking time: 1 hour - Resting time: 1 hour

Ingredients for 4 people:

- 1 chicken (approx. 2¼ lb)
- 10 oz yellow potatoes
- 2 firm ripe tomatoes
- 3½ oz gherkins
- ½ fresh onion
- 1 carrot
- 1 rib celery
- 3 stalks Italian parsley
- 1 bunch radishes
- 1 head romaine lettuce
- 2½ tablespoons desalinated capers
- ½ cup mayonnaise
- 1 cup low-fat Greek yogurt
- 2 hard-boiled eggs
- salt to taste

Preparation:

Heat the water in a saucepan with the celery, carrot, onion and parsley. When it reaches boiling point, add the chicken, previously washed in running water.

Return to the boil, lower the heat and allow to simmer for about an hour. Remove the chicken and place it in a bowl. Cover with plastic wrap and allow to cool. Skin the chicken, bone it and shred the meat.

In the meantime, place the unpeeled potatoes in cold water and boil until tender. Drain and peel when cool. Cut into pieces.

Cut the tomatoes in half and deseed them. Dice, salt and place in a colander to drain.

Slice the gherkins and place them in a salad bowl with the chicken, capers and drained tomatoes.

Place the mayonnaise and yogurt in a bowl and beat to form a creamy sauce. Add to the chicken in the salad bowl and carefully toss all the ingredients together. Season with salt.

Wash the lettuce, keeping only the heart. Dry it with kitchen paper and tear into pieces before adding to the chicken. Decorate with segments of hard-boiled eggs and halved radishes.

Insalata di pollo dello zio Gufo

Cherry
volcano

Preparation time: 15 minutes - Cooking time: 30 minutes - Resting time: 30 minutes

Ingredients for 1 tart:

- 7¼ cups ripe red-purple cherries
- 2 cups all-purpose flour
- ⅞ cup softened salted butter
- 1½ cups turbinado sugar
- confectioner's sugar to taste

Preparation:

Quickly rub the butter into the flour and 1 cup of the turbinado sugar to make a smooth pastry.

Form a ball, cover with plastic wrap and refrigerate for 30 minutes.

Remove the stones from the cherries, place them in a tart pan (9" diameter, 1" deep) and cover with the remaining ½ cup turbinado sugar.

Remove the pastry from the fridge and roll it out into a circle between 2 lightly floured sheets of parchment paper. Place the disc on top of the cherries.

Bake at 400°F for 25 minutes.

Remove from the oven, dredge with confectioner's sugar and return to the oven for 5 more minutes. The center of the pastry crust will crack and sink among the cherries, making it resemble a volcano crater full of molten lava.

Vulcano di ciliegie

Rose aperitif
Crispy lasagne
with ragù and
Parmesan
zabaglione
**Mezze maniche
pasta with
vegetables**
Mother's love
hearts
**Lemon meringue
pie**

Mother's Day

Rose
aperitif

Preparation time: 10 minutes

Ingredients for one 50-oz pitcher:

- 4¼ cups sparkling water (for children)
- 4¼ cups Prosecco or sparkling white wine (for adults)
- ⅔ cup rose syrup
- juice of ½ lemon
- ice cubes to taste

Preparation:

Mix the sparkling water or the Prosecco with the rose syrup in a pitcher.

Add the strained juice of ½ lemon and serve with plenty of ice.

Aperitivo alle rose antiche

Crispy lasagne with ragù and Parmesan zabaglione

Preparation time: 40 minutes - Cooking time: 90 minutes

Ingredients for 4 people:

- 12 squares of egg lasagne (5" x 5")
- ⅔ cup ground pork
- ⅔ cup ground veal
- 1¼ tablespoons tomato paste
- 1 shallot
- 1 garlic clove
- fresh herbs (thyme and marjoram)
- 2 cups vegetable stock (celery, carrot and onion)
- 1 knob of butter
- ¼ cup grated Parmesan cheese
- 1¾ tablespoon extra virgin olive oil
- salt to taste
- pepper to taste

White sauce:
- ½ cup all-purpose flour
- ¼ cup butter
- 2 cups full-cream milk
- nutmeg to taste
- salt to taste
- pepper to taste

Parmesan zabaglione
- 3 very fresc egg yolks
- ½ cup grated Parmesan cheese
- 1 laddle vegetable stock
- white or black pepper to taste

Preparation of ragù:

Heat the oil with the chopped shallot and the unpeeled clove of garlic. Add the ground meat and, after a few minutes, the tomato paste. Cook for at least 30 minutes.

Add a ladle of vegetable stock every now and then, but keep the sauce fairly dry. Finally, add the herbs, season with salt and pepper, and set aside.

Preparation of white sauce:

Melt the butter and add the flour, allow to cook for a few minutes, then add the milk and cook for 10–15 minutes, stirring all the time. Season with salt, pepper and nutmeg. Cover the surface with plastic wrap and set aside.

Preparation of Parmesan zabaglione:

Place the egg yolks, Parmesan cheese and stock in a bain-marie.

Beat with a whisk and then cook, stirring all the time with a wooden spoon, until the zabaglione reaches 180°F. Season to taste with white or black pepper.

Assembly of the dish:

Boil the pasta in plenty of boiling salted water for 20 seconds. Remove and immediately plunge into iced water. Drain on a clean, dry tea towel.

Cut 2 squares into 4 equal parts and leave 4 whole.

Grease 4 disposable crème caramel molds.

Place a whole sheet of pasta in each mold, add a tablespoon of ragù and a tablespoon of Parmesan. Cover with a small sheet of pasta and add a tablespoon of white sauce. Repeat to form three layers.

Seal to form a parcel. Brush with melted butter and sprinkle with Parmesan.

Bake at 350°F for 15 minutes. Remove from the oven and place in a serving bowl lightly sprinkled with the Parmesan sauce.

Lasagne croccanti con ragù
e zabaione di parmigiano

Mezze maniche pasta with vegetables

Preparation time: 20 minutes - Cooking time: 20 minutes

Ingredients for 4 people:

- 3 cups mezze maniche pasta
- 1lb ripe sauce tomatoes
- 1 sweet pepper
- 1 zucchini
- 2 ribs celery
- 2 spring onions
- 2 garlic cloves
- basil to taste
- Italian parsley to taste
- ½ cup grated Pecorino cheese
- 5 tablespoons extra virgin olive oil
- salt to taste

Preparation:

Cut a cross on the bottom of the tomatoes and plunge them into boiling water for a few seconds. Drain and place in a boil of cold water. Peel and cut into segments. Remove the seeds and dice. Set aside.

Wash, trim and dice all the other vegetables.

In a frying pan, sauté the spring onions with a tablespoon of oil and set aside.

After removing the spring onions, sauté the slightly crushed unpeeled cloves of garlic in the same pan and add the diced pepper.

When cooked, add to the spring onions.

Remove the garlic from the pan and add a tablespoon of water. Deglaze and stir the juices into the peppers and spring onions.

Mezze maniche
alle verdure

Repeat the process with the zucchini and the celery. Add the fresh basil and parsley.

In the meantime, cook the pasta in plenty of boiling salted water, drain and sauté for a few seconds with the vegetables and the diced tomatoes.

Arrange a layer of pasta in a ovenproof dish and sprinkle with a handful of Pecorino cheese. Repeat, ending with the Pecorino. Cover with a tea towel and allow to rest for 5 minutes. Drizzle over the remaining olive oil, mix well and serve.

Mother's love hearts

Preparation time: 30 minutes - Cooking time: 20 minutes - Resting time: 60 minutes

Ingredients for 12 cookies:

Cookies:
- 3 cups all-purpose flour
- 1 egg
- ⅔ cup softened butter
- ⅔ cup sugar

Colored caramel:
- ⅞ cup water
- 2⅔ cup sugar
- ½ cup glucose
- red food coloring

Preparation:

Beat the egg, add the sugar and mix in the butter and the flour. Beat until smooth and form the dough into a ball. Cover with plastic wrap and refrigerate for 30 minutes.

Roll out to a thickness of at least ¼" and cut out cookies using a heart-shaped cutter.

Place on a baking sheet lined with parchment paper and bake at 350°F for 20 minutes.

Allow to cool and set aside.

Mix the water, sugar and glucose in a pan. Heat to a temperature of 305°F without stirring. Remove from the heat and add the food coloring, stirring gently.

Using tongs, dip the cookies in the caramel, taking care to coat them completely. Allow to drain for a few moments, then place the cookies on parchment paper and allow the caramel to set.

Cuor d'amore per la mamma

Lemon
meringue pie

Preparation time: 60 minutes - Cooking time: 25 minutes for the pie
Resting time: 30 minutes for the pastry + 15 minutes

Ingredients for 8 people:

Shortcrust pastry:
- 3 cups all-purpose flour
- ⅔ cup chilled salted butter, diced
- 1 egg
- 1¾ tablespoons water
- 2 tablespoons superfine sugar
- ½ teaspoon salt

Lemon custard:
- 2¼ cups fresh milk
- 4 egg yolks
- ¾ cup superfine sugar
- ⅜ cup all-purpose flour
- vanilla pod
- juice and grated zest of ½ organic lemon

Meringue:
- 4 egg whites
- 3½ tablespoons water
- 1⅓ cup superfine sugar
- 2½ tablespoons confectioner's sugar

Preparation of shortcrust pastry:

In a large bowl, rub the butter into the flour with your fingertips until the mixture resembles coarse breadcrumbs.

Make a well and place the water, sugar, salt and egg in the center.

Knead until the pastry is smooth.

Roll into a ball, cover with plastic wrap and refrigerate for 30 minutes.

Preparation of lemon custard:

Cut the vanilla pod lengthwise and boil it in the milk.

Beat the egg yolks with the sugar and add the sifted flour.

Add the hot milk and mix well.

Return to the heat and boil for a few minutes. Remove from the stove and add the lemon juice and zest.

Cover the surface with plastic wrap and allow to cool.

Preparation of pastry case:

Roll out the pastry between two sheets of parchment paper in order to avoid adding extra flour. Prick the pastry disc with a fork.

With the help of a rolling pin, place the pastry in a greased tart pan, pricked side uppermost, and trim the edges. Refrigerate for 15 minutes.

Remove from the fridge and cover with a circle of parchment paper. Cover the base with pie weights or dried legumes and bake in a preheated oven at 350°F for 20 minutes. Remove the pie weights and allow to cook for a further 10 minutes.

Leave to cool.

Preparation of meringue:

While the pastry case is baking, prepare the meringue.

Whip the egg whites with a teaspoon of sugar until stiff.

Put the remaining sugar in a saucepan with the water, heat to 250°F and remove from the heat.

Pour slowly onto the egg whites, whisking until they form peaks.

Fold one third of the meringue mixture into the lemon custard.

Preparation of pie:

Place the lemon custard mixture on the base of the pie and cover with the meringue, using your fingers to form peaks. Sprinkle with the confectioner's sugar and place under a hot grill until the meringue is golden (max. 2 minutes).

Crostata con crema di limone e meringa

Father's Day

Elderflower aperitif
Pesto gnocchi with roasted cherry tomatoes
Chickpea and maltagliati pasta soup
Meaty flying saucers
Chicken drumsticks with roast potatoes and peas
Tiramisu with candy-coated chocolate drops

Elderflower aperitif

Preparation time: 10 minutes

Ingredients for one 50-oz pitcher:

- 4¼ cups sparkling water (for children)
- 4¼ cups Prosecco or sparkling white wine (for adults)
- ⅔ cup elderflower syrup
- juice of ½ lemon
- 4 fresh mint leaves
- ice cubes to taste

Preparation:

In a pitcher, mix the elderflower syrup with the sparkling water or the Prosecco, adding the strained juice of ½ lemon and the mint leaves.

Serve with plenty of ice.

Aperitivo ai fiori
di sambuco

Pesto gnocchi with roasted cherry tomatoes

Preparation time: 90 minutes - Cooking time: 60 minutes - Resting time: 30 minutes

Ingredients for 4 people:

Gnocchi:
- 2¼ lb white potatoes, preferably old
- 1½-2 cups all-purpose flour

Genoese pesto:
- 40 Ligurian basil leaves
- 1 garlic clove, peeled
- ¼ cup grated Parmesan cheese
- ⅛ cup grated Pecorino Sardo cheese
- ¼ cup pine nuts
- 5 tablespoons mild extra virgin olive oil
- salt to taste

Roasted cherry tomatoes:
- 20 cherry tomatoes
- 3 tablespoons extra virgin olive oil
- salt to taste
- pepper to taste

Preparation of gnocchi:

Line a baking sheet with 2 lb coarse salt. Wrap the washed potatoes in foil, dull side outwards. Make a hole in the foil with a knife and arrange the potatoes hole side down on the baking sheet. Bake at 300°F for approximately 40 minutes, until the potatoes are cooked.

Remove the potatoes from the oven and discard the foil. Peel and mash. Leave to cool.

Pile the mashed potato onto a pastry board, make a well in the center and add the flour to it. Knead the mixture, adding flour until it no longer sticks to your hands.

When the dough is smooth and elastic, break off a piece and roll it on the lightly floured pastry board to form a long sausage as thick as your finger. Cut into 1" pieces.

Roll each of the gnocchi over the back of a grater or a fork, pressing lightly with your thumb. Allow them to drop onto a floured tea towel, taking care that they don't stick together.

Gnocchi al pesto con pomodorini al forno

When you have finished, cover them with another tea towel and allow to rest for not more than 30 minutes.

Preparation of pesto:

If you don't have the traditional marble mortar with olivewood pestle, use a blender that you have put in the freezer (complete with blade) for at least 2 hours. This will prevent the basil from oxidizing and turning black.

Place the basil leaves in the blender with the crushed garlic, salt and half the oil and whizz on the lowest speed setting.

Add the pine nuts, cheeses and the rest of the oil and increase the speed, pausing frequently, until obtaining a smooth, creamy, bright green sauce.

Preparation of cherry tomatoes:

Wash the tomatoes and cut in half. Place them on parchment paper, cut side uppermost. Season with salt and pepper and drizzle with olive oil. Roast at 50°F for approximately 20 minutes.

Assembly of the dish:

Cook the gnocchi in plenty of boiling salted water and remove with a slotted spoon as soon as they surface. Arrange in a deep serving dish, pour over the pesto and add the roasted tomatoes.

Chickpea and maltagliati pasta soup

Preparation time: 60 minutes - Cooking time: 40 minutes

Ingredients for 4 people:

Maltagliati pasta:
- 3 cups all-purpose flour
- 3 medium fresh eggs

Chickpea soup
- 2½ cups dried chickpeas, soaked
- 1 onion
- 2 garlic cloves
- 1 rib celery
- 1 sprig rosemary
- 1 stalk parsley
- a few sage leaves
- 4¼ cups vegetable stock (celery, carrot and onion)
- extra virgin olive oil
- salt to taste
- pepper to taste

Preparation of maltagliati pasta:

Form a mound with the flour on a pastry board, make a well in the center and place all the eggs in it. Beat the eggs with a fork and mix in the flour, taking care not to break the sides of the well.

When the mixture starts to thicken, continue with your hands, taking care to incorporate all the flour (use a spatula to help you). Knead well until the dough is smooth and elastic. To check if the dough is ready, cut in half: the inside should be spongy with air bubbles.

Cover the dough with plastic wrap until you roll it out. Use a rolling pin or a pasta machine to roll out the pasta to the size of a sheet of lasagne. It should not be too thin. Cut into lozenges, set aside on a floured chopping board and cover with a tea towel.

Zuppa di ceci e maltagliati

Preparation of soup:

Remove the stalks from the parsley and the rosemary and chop the leaves with the onion, celery and 1 peeled clove of garlic. Sauté in a large pan with 2 tablespoons of oil.

Add the drained chickpeas, cover with the vegetable stock and allow to simmer for about 40 minutes until the chickpeas are tender. Season with salt and pepper to taste.

Drain half of the chickpeas and whizz in a blender, then force through a medium-mesh sieve to remove the skins.

Put the sage and 1 slightly crushed unpeeled clove of garlic in a saucepan with 3 tablespoons of oil. Add the puréed chickpeas and cook over a low heat for 10 minutes.

Bring the pan with the whole chickpeas back to the boil and add the maltagliati pasta. Season with salt and add the puréed chickpeas 3 minutes before the end of cooking.

Serve hot.

Meaty flying saucers

Preparation time: 30 minutes - Cooking time: 15 minutes - Rising time: 90 minutes

Ingredients for 4 people (8 mini burgers):
- 8 honey and sesame rolls (1 oz each)
- 1½ cups lean ground beef
- mayonnaise to taste
- ketchup to taste

Honey and sesame rolls:
- 1¾ cups all-purpose flour
- 1¾ cups bread flour
- ½ tablespoon brewer's yeast
- 1 whole egg and 2 yolks + 1 yolk for glazing
- ¾ cup milk
- ½ cup water
- 3 tablespoons honey
- ¼ cup softened butter
- sesame seeds
- 1 teaspoon salt

Preparation of honey and sesame rolls:

Dissolve the yeast in the water.

Gently beat the eggs together with the honey and add to the water.

Add the two types of flour and mix well. Knead to form a smooth dough, then add the salt and, finally, the softened butter. Allow the mixture to rise until doubled in size (approximately 60 minutes).

Divide the dough into portions weighing about 1 oz each and allow to rise again until the individual rolls have doubled in size (approximately 30 minutes).

Glaze the rolls with the egg yolk mixed with milk and sprinkle with the sesame seeds. Bake at 350°F for 5–10 minutes.

Preparation of burgers:

Shape the meat into evenly sized balls, flatten them and then cook in a cast-iron frying pan.

Cut the bread rolls in half, spread mayonnaise on one side and ketchup on the other, and place the burgers in the middle.

WILL
PAPÀ

Chicken drumsticks with roast potatoes and peas

Preparation time: 30 + 15 + 30 minutes - Cooking time: 60 + 50 + 15 minutes

Ingredients for 4 people:

- 1¼ lb chicken drumsticks
- 1¼ lb firm yellow potatoes
- 1¼ lb tender baby peas
- 2 spring onions
- 5 garlic cloves
- 1 sprig rosemary
- 4 large tender leaves sage
- 2 cups vegetable stock
- ½ cup dry white wine
- ¼ cup white vinegar
- 8 tablespoons extra virgin olive oil
- sugar to taste
- salt to taste
- pepper to taste

Preparation:

Wash and dry the chicken drumsticks.

Sauté the drumsticks with 2 tablespoons of olive oil in a wide pan. Season with salt and pepper and continue cooking until golden all over.

Peel 2 cloves of garlic and chop finely with the sage and rosemary leaves.

Sprinkle the chopped herbs over the drumsticks, reduce the heat and allow flavors to mingle, mixing well.

In the meantime, boil the wine with the vinegar over a high heat for several minutes to remove the alcohol.

Pour the wine and vinegar over the chicken and continue to cook, periodically basting with the juices and, if it starts to dry out, with a little vegetable stock.

While the chicken finishes cooking, cut the potatoes into dice or evenly sized segments. Wash and dry thoroughly with a tea towel.

In a large roasting pan, heat 5 tablespoons of olive oil and add the potatoes in a single layer, turning to ensure that they are completely coated. Season with salt and pepper, add 3 slightly crushed unpeeled cloves of garlic and roast at 400°F for 45–50 minutes. Every now and then, turn the potatoes with a fish slice, taking care not to break them.

Discard the roots and green parts of the spring onions, then chop very finely. Sauté in the oil in a frying pan over a medium heat, taking care not to let them brown. Add the shelled peas and stir well. Season with salt and a pinch of superfine sugar, then add a ladle of hot vegetable stock.

Cover the pan and continue to cook over a medium heat until the peas are tender.

Serve the chicken drumsticks with the peas and potatoes.

Cosce di pollo con patate arrosto e piselli

Tiramisu with candy-coated chocolate drops

Preparation time: 90 minutes - Cooking time: 30 minutes - Resting time: 2 hours

Ingredients for 4 people:

- ½ lb sponge
- ⅔ cup egg yolks (approx. 10 eggs)
- ½ cup mascarpone cheese
- ½ cup cream
- 1½ cups superfine sugar
- ⅜ cup water
- ½ cup colored candy-coated chocolate drops
- ⅔ cup cocoa powder

Barley coffee syrup:
- 10 tablespoons instant barley coffee
- ⅔ cup superfine sugar
- ⅞ cup water

Sponge:
- 1¾ cups all-purpose flour
- 4 eggs
- ¾ cup superfine sugar + extra for dusting
- confectioner's sugar for dusting

Preparation of pasteurized tiramisu base:

Heat the water and sugar to 250°F in a small saucepan. Lightly beat the egg yolks in a food mixer with the whisk attachment, then slowly add the boiling water and sugar mixture, beating all the time. Continue to whisk on high speed until the mixture is cool.

Preparation of classic tiramisu cream:

Whisk the mascarpone cheese into the pasteurized tiramisu base, then add the lightly whipped cream.

Preparation of sponge:

Beat the egg yolks with the superfine sugar in a food mixer with the whisk attachment until the mixture is smooth but not too thick. Whisk the egg whites separately until stiff and set aside.

Fold the flour into the egg yolks using a spatula, then fold in the egg whites, always using a downward movement to avoid knocking the air out of the mixture. Spread the mixture over a baking sheet lined with parchment paper, dust with confectioner's sugar and superfine sugar and bake in a preheated oven at 450°F for about 7 minutes.

Preparation of barley coffee syrup:

Mix all the ingredients together in a saucepan and heat to a temperature of 185°F. Allow to cool to room temperature

Assembly of the tiramisu:

Alternate layers of sponge dipped in the barley coffee syrup with the cream, ending with a layer of cream. Refrigerate for at least 2 hours. Dust with the cocoa powder and decorate with the colored candy-coated chocolate drops.

Tiramisù con i bottoni di cioccolata

Santa Claus is coming!

Christmas tree cookies
Fizzy chocolate and dried fruit and nut medallions
Cinnamon stars
Transparent spheres with fruit jellies
Grandma Maria's chocolate pots
Salted caramel pots
Aromatic salt
Desert roses
Auntie Chiara's marmalade

Christmas tree cookies

Preparation time: 60 minutes - Cooking time: 15 minutes - Resting time: 30 minutes

Ingredients for 15 medium cookies:

Cookie dough:
- 3 cups all-purpose flour
- 1⅓ cups softened butter
- ⅔ cup superfine sugar
- 1 egg

Icing:
- 2⅛ cup confectioner's sugar
- 1½ tablespoons egg whites
- 1⅓ tablespoons lemon juice

Preparation of cookies:

Quickly mix together all the cookie dough ingredients until smooth. Form into a ball, cover with plastic wrap and refrigerate for 30 minutes.

Place the dough between 2 sheets of parchment paper and roll out to a thickness of ¾".

Use tree-shaped cutters to make the biscuits.

Preparation of icing:

Sift the sugar into a bowl, add the egg whites and the lemon juice and beat with an electric whisk until thick and fluffy.

Divide the icing into separate bowls, adding food coloring of your choice to each.

Cover the surface of the icing with plastic wrap to prevent it setting.

Ice the cookies when cool.

Fizzy chocolate and dried fruit and nut medallions

Preparation time: 20 minutes - Resting time: 20 minutes

Ingredients for 10 chocolates:

- 7 oz dark chocolate
- 1 oz white chocolate (or 9 oz milk chocolate if preferred)
- 2 walnut kernels
- 2 hazelnuts
- 2 small sticks candied ginger
- 1 tablespoon dried coconut
- 1 tablespoon raisins
- 1 tablespoon Frizzi (paste acidifier)

Preparation:

Melt the dark and white chocolate together in a bain-marie.

Chop the nuts, raisins and ginger and mix with the dried coconut.

Pour a small amount of chocolate into silicone medallion molds, add the fruit and nut mixture and the Frizzi and refrigerate for 20 minutes.

Remove excess topping and unmold the chocolates.

Medaglioni frizzanti di cioccolato con frutta secca

Cinnamon
stars

Preparation time: 60 minutes - Resting time: 6-12 hours - Cooking time: 3–5 minutes

Ingredients for 50 stars:

- 4 cups ground almonds
- 2 egg whites
- 2 cups confectioner's sugar
- 1 tablespoon ground cinnamon
- ½ tablespoon lemon juice

Tip:
The cinnamon stars can be placed
in tins and given to teachers.

Preparation:

Place the egg whites in a bowl with
the confectioner's sugar and whip
with an electric whisk. Set aside
3½ oz of the mixture to ice the stars.

Fold the ground almonds, lemon
juice and cinnamon into the
remaining mixture until smooth.

Roll out the dough to a thickness of
¼" on a flat surface sprinkled with
superfine sugar.

Use cutters to make stars and place
them on a baking sheet lined with
parchment paper.

Allow to dry out, preferably
overnight, at room temperature.

The following day, bake the stars at
400°F for 3–5 minutes and dip the
upper sides quickly into the icing
while still hot.

Transparent spheres with fruit jellies

Preparation time: 40 minutes - Resting time: 30 minutes

Ingredients for 24 jellies:

- 2 cups strained fresh pink grapefruit (or orange) juice or 2¼ cups puréed blackberry juice, filtered through a fine strainer
- 1¼ teaspoons water
- ⅓ cup glucose (½ cup for blackberry)
- 1 tablespoon pectin (+¼ teaspoon for blackberry)
- 1½ teaspoons cream of tartar
- ⅛ cup superfine sugar (¼ cup for blackberry)
- 1¾ cups coarse sugar (2½ cups for blackberry) + extra for dusting

Preparation:

Bring the grapefruit (or orange or blackberry) juice to the boil.

Mix the pectin with the superfine sugar and stir into the boiling fruit juice, adding the glucose and coarse sugar. Cook at 225°F, stirring regularly.

When the mixture is cooked, dissolve the cream of tartar in the water and stir into the jelly.

Pour into molds and allow to set.

Remove from the moulds and roll in coarse sugar before serving.

Sfere trasparenti con gelatine di frutta

222

Grandma Maria's chocolate pots

Preparation time: 15 minutes - Cooking time: 20 minutes

Ingredients for 6 small jars:

- 7 oz dark chocolate
- ¾ cup superfine sugar
- ½ cup fresh cream
- ¼ cup butter

Preparation:

Melt the chocolate with the butter in a bain-marie.

Heat the cream with the sugar,

Add the hot cream to the melted chocolate and fill the jars.

Allow to cool before sealing the jars.

Vasetto di cioccolata come quello di nonna Maria

Salted
caramel pots

Preparation time: 15 minutes - Cooking time: 20 minutes

Ingredients for 6 small jars:

- 2 cups superfine sugar
- ⅞ cup water
- ½ cup salted butter
- 2 cups whipping cream

Preparation:

In a small pan, heat the water with the sugar without stirring and cook until golden.

Heat the cream and add the chopped butter.

When the caramel is clear and golden, add the hot cream and butter mixture. Cook until achieving the desired consistency.

Pour into the jars and allow to cool before sealing.

Vasetto con salsa mou salata

Aromatic salt

Preparation time: 20 minutes

Ingredients for 6 jars:

- 2 cups coarse salt
- 1 organic orange
- 1 garlic clove
- 1 sprig fresh thyme
- 1 sprig rosemary
- 2 leaves sage

Tip:
This salt can be used to flavor your dishes. Lemon peel can be used in place of orange peel if preferred. Lightly toasted sesame seeds can be added. It can still be used after the oxidation and darkening of the herbs.

Preparation:

Peel the orange with a potato peeler, taking care to remove the white pith.

Put all the ingredients in a blender and whizz for a few minutes.

Store in an airtight jar in the fridge and use within 7 days.

Vasetto con sale aromatico

Desert roses

Preparation time: 20 minutes - Cooking time: 5 minutes - Resting time: 30 minutes

Ingredients for 10 roses:
- 4 cups cornflakes
- 2¾ oz dark chocolate
- 3 oz milk chocolate
- 3½ oz white chocolate

Tip:
The desert roses can be placed in tins and given to teachers.

Preparation:
Melt the three different kinds of chocolate separately in a bain-marie

Place the cornflakes in a bowl, add all the chocolate and mix gently.

Fill paper cake cases with the chocolate-covered cornflakes and refrigerate for 30 minutes.

Auntie Chiara's marmalade

Resting time: 1–3 days - Preparation time: 60 minutes - Cooking time: 3 hours

Ingredients for 2 medium jars:
- 6 thin-skinned oranges
- 1 large lemon
- sugar according to weight

Preparation:

Wash the oranges and the lemon thoroughly and cut into thin slices, discarding the ends.

Place the citrus slices in a large bowl and add 5¾ cups water for each lb of fruit. Cover and allow to rest for 1–3 days.

Pour into a saucepan and cook over a high heat for approximately 1 hour, until the peels are tender.

Allow to cool and add ½ lb sugar for each lb of fruit mixture.

Return to the stove and cook for a couple of hours, until a spoonful of syrup poured onto a saucer sets without spreading.

Pour the boiling marmalade into the jars and seal immediately.

Keep in the fridge and use within one month.

Vasetto con marmellata di arance come quella di zia Chiara

Index of recipes

Maria Castellano

Swiss born (1969), Milanese by adoption and Roman at heart, Maria is a freelancer who works with leading Italian chefs and teaches in prestigious cookery schools. These include Aurelio Carraffa's *Mediterraneum* and *Eataly* in Rome; *Gli Amici di Babette* in Bologna, where she teaches bread and pastry making; *Eataly* in Turin; the *Gambero Rosso* schools in Rome; and recently also the cookery school held aboard the MSC cruise ships and sponsored by *Gente* magazine. Her first book, *Pane & Co.* was published in 2010 by Bibliotheca Culinaria.

Stefano Scatà

Born in Pordenone in 1956, following an arts degree from Bologna University, Stefano became a photographer in 1984 and has worked for the leading Italian and international magazines. He specializes in travel photojournalism, paying particular attention to lifestyle. A great food lover, he soon came into contact with the world of food and everything in its orbit. The resulting books, in which the eye of the camera captures the soul of its subject with great simplicity, are characterized by great enthusiasm and freshness.

Monica Parussolo

Born in Treviso (1984), Monica studied at the Academy of Fine Arts in Venice, specializing in the teaching of art. She studied comic strips and illustration in Bologna and Sarmede, while becoming in expert in the work of Bruno Munari. She expresses herself principally with the forms and materials typical of childhood: stamps, colored and crumpled paper, textures, rubbings, colored masks and small everyday objects, giving her images that astonished quality that characterizes the world of each child.